Winemaking with Concentrates

D1639256

Winemaking with Concentrates

PETER DUNCAN

NEXUS SPECIAL INTERESTS

Nexus Special Interests Ltd
Nexus House
Boundary Way
Hemel Hempstead
Herts HP2 7ST
England

First published 1976
Second edition 1982
Reprinted 1995

ISBN 1-85486-118-2

Design and typesetting by The Studio, Exeter
Printed and bound in Great Britain by Biddles Ltd, Guildford & King's Lynn

CONTENTS

Chapter 1	Basic Principles and Practices	1
	Equipment	2
	The Hydrometer	9
	Gravity Tables	13
	Cleaning and Sterilizing	14
	Yeast	16
	Yeast Starters	17
	Yeast Nutrients	18
	Fermentation	19
	Acid Balance	20
	Tannin	21
	Racking and Clarification	23
	Maturing	25
	Spoilage	27
Chapter 2	Grape Concentrate	29
	Practical Aspects	34
	Production of Grape Concentrate Wine	39
Chapter 3	Frozen and Canned Fruit Concentrates	41
Chapter 4	A Range of Recipes	45
	Index	88

CHAPTER 1

Basic Principles and Practices

Introduction

There must be few wine lovers indeed who have not heard or read about the pleasant and enjoyable wines which can nowadays be produced from grape and other fruit juice concentrates, and many have already tried their hand at making their own wine in this simple modern manner. Admittedly, wine made in this way can hardly be compared with that from the best châteaux of Bordeaux, but it can certainly compete very favourably in quality with many imported wines and has the great advantage of costing much less. The fact that there are several highly successful domestic wineries producing their wine commercially from grape concentrate merely goes to confirm how good wine made from concentrate really can be.

The rate at which world prices for wine have been rising in recent years has meant that many families who formerly enjoyed wine regularly with their meals can now do so only on special occasions. Although it may no longer be feasible for them to buy wine every day, it is so easy and inexpensive to make it from grape concentrate that there should never be any risk of their wine cellar running dry.

Some guidance is nevertheless necessary no mattter how simple it may be to make wine from concentrate and allied ingredients. The following sections are therefore devoted to a brief review of the basic winemaking principles and practices which should always be observed whenever wine is made.

1

Equipment

It is often claimed that wine can be successfully produced at home using nothing but equipment which can already be found in the kitchen, whereas in actual fact it is rather naive to believe that this is really the case. Many common household items can certainly be pressed into service, e.g. scales, wooden spoons, nylon strainers, etc., but even the best equipped kitchen is unlikely to have anything in the way of large glass carboys, fermentation locks, lengths of siphon tubing and so on! The budding winemaker should consequently be prepared to spend a few pounds to acquire certain basic pieces of equipment which experience has shown to be almost indispensable for the production of good wine with the least expenditure of time and effort.

A word of warning is perhaps advisable at this point before beginning to describe what equipment to buy for the wine cellar. Metal articles should be avoided at all costs because wines are slightly acid and will dissolve small amounts of most metals allowed to come into contact with them. Contamination by metal is both undesirable and potentially dangerous. Not only can minute quantities of metal in a wine cause persistent hazes and peculiar off-flavours, but in the case of lead its presence can actually render the wine poisonous. It is therefore merely a matter of common sense to resolve never to use anything metallic for winemaking activities.

First on the list of essential equipment comes a primary fermentation vessel which is basically just a large wide-mouthed container. At one time, earthenware crocks were favoured for this purpose, but they suffer from the disadvantages of being heavy, expensive and easily broken. In addition, many old containers of this sort and, incredible as it may seem, some of quite recent manufacture have been glazed with lead salts. Since wine will extract lead from this type of glaze and instances of lead poisoning due to drinking wine containing lead derived from this very source are occasionally reported in the press, it is clearly safer to leave earthenware vessels alone insofar as winemaking is concerned.

The modern winemaker employs plastic containers resembling plastic dustbins as primary fermentation vessels, but some care should be exercised in their selection. Conventional plastic dustbins can in fact serve as primary fermentation vessels and have the advantage of being relatively cheap. Unfortunately, their tendency to split at an inconvenient moment and spill their contents all over the floor does not

Plastic primary fermentation vessels in natural (uncoloured) high density polyethylene.

commend their use for this purpose. Some winemakers also feel that toxic pigments sometimes employed as colouring agents for these products may pose a hazard if they serve as fermentation vessels for wine.

It is far better to pay a little extra to buy a proper primary fermentation vessel which will be manufactured from natural (uncoloured) high density polyethylene or polypropylene, will have extra-thick walls and will be altogether more rugged in construction. The 8-10 gallon (35-45 litres) size is recommended for the production of wine in batches of 5-6 gallons (20-25 litres) while a 2 gallon (10 litres) plastic pail of the same type is excellent for making single gallons (5 litres) at a time.

Although this type of primary fermentation vessel can normally be put into service after rinsing it out with water and sterilizing it because it has been approved for use in the food industry, the same cannot be said for ordinary plastic dustbins. Many of the latter retain a thin but

3

tenacious film of a substance applied to the mould in which they were formed to facilitate their release from it. Since this material will dissolve in the wine during fermentation and would render it quite undrinkable, it must obviously be removed before such containers are ready to hold wine.

The answer to this problem is to wipe the interior of the vessel with a cloth soaked in rubbing alcohol or methyl hydrate, which any reputable chemist or ironmonger will stock. It should next be washed thoroughly with hot soapy water and then rinsed once or twice with cold water. This treatment will effectively remove any mould release agent adhering to the plastic and will at the same time sterilize the container so that it is ready for immediate use.

The next indispensable item which is not found in the average kitchen is a large narrow-necked container such as a glass carboy or gallon jar to serve as a secondary fermentation vessel. The reason why both a primary and a secondary fermentation vessel are required is really quite simple and extremely practical. As will be explained later, during what is called the primary fermentation (which to all intents and purposes means during the initial 5-8 days after the yeast was added), a great deal of frothing and foaming commonly occurs. This phase of the fermentation must therefore be conducted in a container with ample head space to ensure that nothing foams over and makes a mess.

Secondary fermentation vessels in glass and plastic: a 'cubitainer', a glass carboy and an Italian demi-john.

Once this vigorous first stage is over, fermentation subsequently proceeds relatively quietly and sedately with little or no froth and foam forming. When this point is reached, it becomes desirable to transfer the fermenting must, as the future wine is called, into a narrow-necked container, for reasons which will become clear shortly.

Glass carboys or demi-johns make ideal secondary fermentation vessels. Although these containers can be obtained in all sizes ranging from 1 gallon (5 litres) all the way up to monsters holding 15 gallons (65 litres) or more, there can be no doubt that those with a capacity of 1 gallon (5 litres) and 5 gallons (25 litres) are the most popular. The preference for these two sizes reflects the fact that most winemakers feel that wine is most easily and conveniently produced in batches of either 1 gallon (5 litres) or 5 gallons (25 litres), and experience certainly supports this view.

Plastic containers can also be useful as secondary fermentation vessels. Collapsible types such as the "ex-wine five" either with or without a supporting cardboard outer are often advocated for this purpose because they are cheaper than glass and virtually unbreakable. These remarks are certainly quite valid and plastic containers of this type undoubtedly are excellent as secondary fermentation vessels. Unfortunately, they are made from low density polyethylene which is permeable to air and so they are unsuitable for storage purposes. Wine kept in them for more than a few weeks absorbs too much oxygen through the walls of the container and rapidly becomes flat and oxidized. Rigid plastic containers fabricated from medium density or high density polyethylene which are less permeable to air are considerably better in this respect, but wines stored in them still need to be inspected regularly to ensure that they do not become over-oxidized.

By way of contrast, glass containers are quite impermeable to air so that they not only function as excellent secondary fermentation vessels but are also equally as good for storing wine. To avoid occupying a valuable carboy in this way, however, it is advisable to acquire some clear or amber gallon (5 litre) jars or wine bottles into which wine can be transferred once fermentation has ceased and clarification is well advanced. The carboy is thus freed for the fermentation of another batch of wine.

Wine which is decanted before serving need not be elaborately bottled and labelled unless the winemaker feels so inclined. A selection of corks, labels, corking equipment and so on would then be required, but these are best regarded as non-essential items to be purchased later as the occasion may demand.

A simpler approach is to store the wine in gallon (5 litre) jars which are emptied one at a time as wine is required into enough standard wine bottles to hold the entire gallon (5 litres). When the last of these bottles is finished, they are simply refilled from a fresh gallon (5 litre) jar and so the process continues. This procedure ensures that the wine is not left too long in a partly filled container and so minimizes the risk of spoilage.

The mouth of a primary or secondary fermentation vessel must be covered to prevent fruit flies, dust and airborne spoilage organisms from gaining access to the fermenting must. Since large volumes of a harmless gas called carbon dioxide are given off during fermentation, the container must obviously be closed with a device which will also allow this gas to escape. This objective can be accomplished very simply in the case of primary fermentation vessels merely by covering them closely with a clean cloth held in place by a large rubber band cut from an old inner tube or by a piece of string.

Although secondary fermentation vessels can be treated in exactly the same fashion, it is preferable to seal them with an ingenious yet simple piece of equipment called a fermentation lock, otherwise known as an air lock, fermentation trap or even as a "bubbler". The latter name is derived from the fact that most air locks permit the carbon dioxide generated during fermentation to bubble out through a water seal. Since there are many ways of achieving this end — there are many different types of fermentation locks, and most of them seem to perform very satisfactorily — it is therefore a matter of personal preference which design the winemaker chooses to use. The only point worth making in this connection is perhaps to note that glass locks are more fragile than plastic ones.

The narrow necks of secondary fermentation vessels make it difficult to fill them without spilling any must or wine unless the latter is poured in through a large plastic funnel. The small funnels which are found in most kitchens may be satisfactory for filling bottles, but they are totally inadequate when it comes to carboys, so that it pays to buy an extra large size for the wine cellar. Funnels fitted with strainers should be viewed with suspicion, for the screen with which they are equipped is often constructed from copper or brass mesh and could cause problems later due to metal contamination.

When transferring wine from one container to another e.g. from a secondary fermentation vessel into gallon (5 litre) jars or bottles for storage, it is easier and less strenuous to do so by siphoning the wine rather than by pouring or decanting it. Siphoning is also better for the well being of the wine because it aerates it to a much lesser extent. While there are many good proprietary wine siphons on the market a length of flexible plastic tubing with an internal diameter of ⅜ inch (9mm) and 5-6 feet (2 metres) long is just as reliable and much cheaper.

It is also a good idea to obtain a J-tube to attach to the piece of siphon tubing. A J-tube is simply a length of glass or rigid plastic tubing with one end slightly curved so that it resembles the letter J in appearance. It is slipped on one end of the siphon tubing and helps to avoid disturbing the sediment when the wine is being siphoned.

These few pieces of equipment are all that are really needed to start making wine at home. Any other items which may be required such as plastic buckets, measuring cups and spoons and the like are standard

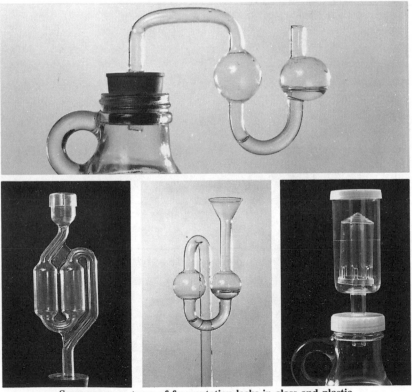

Some common types of fermentation locks in glass and plastic.

The technique of racking.

kitchen utensils which can be pressed into service for winemaking too. Later on, after gaining more experience and confidence, the winemaker may wish to acquire a thermometer, bottle brushes and similar useful accessories, but for the time being there is little in favour of going to the extra expense their purchase would entail.

The Hydrometer

One item of equipment which has not been included in the preceding list is the hydrometer. The reason for this omission is very simply that most winemakers consider the hydrometer to be so important an instrument in the wine cellar that it deserves a section all to itself.

In appearance, the hydrometer is a closed glass cylinder weighted at the base to make it float upright and narrowing at the top into a long, slender glass tube bearing a graduated scale. The accompanying illustration shows what a hydrometer really looks like far better than words can describe it.

The purpose of the hydrometer is to measure the specific gravity of liquids which means that it shows how much lighter or heavier they are than water. In practice, enough of the must or wine being tested is poured into a glass or plastic trial jar to fill it to within an inch or so of the top. The hydrometer is then carefully inserted into the liquid in the trial jar, released to find its own level and spun gently to dislodge any bubbles clinging to it. The reading on the graduated scale at the point where the liquid cuts the stem gives the specific gravity of the must or wine.

The specific gravity of a must can provide the winemaker with a tremendous amount of valuable information. Pure water has by definition a specific gravity of 1.000, but when it contains dissolved substances like sugar their presence has the effect of increasing its specific gravity. Since the actual specific gravity of the solution depends upon how much sugar it contains, it is a very easy matter to calculate the amount of sugar in a must just by measuring its specific gravity.

Once the winemaker has determined the specific gravity of the must with the hydrometer, its sugar content can immediately be established by referring to an appropriate set of tables such as appear on page 13 of this book. It can then be seen at a glance that a must with a specific gravity of 1.050 contains 19 ozs. sugar per gallon (123 gms. per litre).

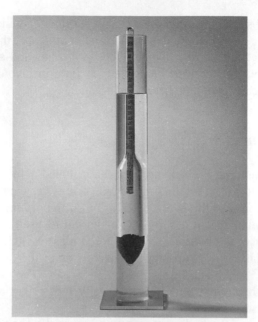

Hydrometer and plastic trial jar.

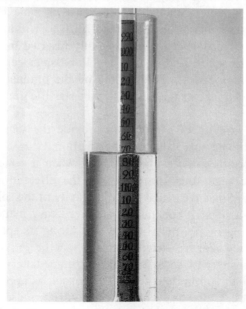

Close-up view showing the gravity reading.

10

In actual fact, for winemaking purposes, it is more usual to refer to the gravity of a must than to its specific gravity. These two terms are really only slightly different ways of expressing the same thing, for the gravity of a must is found by subtracting the specific gravity of water (1.000) from its measured specific gravity and disregarding the decimal point. For example, the must with the specific gravity of 1.050 mentioned previously has a gravity of 50.

Since about half of the total amount of sugar present in a must is converted into alcohol during fermentation, the alcoholic strength of a wine can be predicted in advance if the weight of the sugar consumed by the yeast is known. In addition to showing how much sugar there is in a must of known gravity, the table on page 13 also has a column entitled "Potential Alcohol, % by vol." The entries under this heading indicate how much alcohol a wine will contain if the yeast ferments all the sugar initially present in the must and the wine ends up dry.

It is still possible to calculate the alcohol content of a wine with the aid of the hydrometer even when fermentation does not yield a dry wine and some sugar remains to sweeten it. The winemaker must first establish the total gravity decrease sustained during fermentation by subtracting the final gravity of the wine from the initial gravity of the must (after allowing for any dilution or sugar additions which may have taken place). The approximate alcoholic strength of the wine can then be estimated by dividing this gravity drop by 7.5. For example, if a must had an initial gravity of 105 and the wine finished up with a gravity of 15, the total drop would be 90. On dividing 90 by 7.5, the wine is found to contain about 12% alcohol by volume.

Dry wines have a final specific gravity slightly below 1.000 because alcohol is lighter than water, so that a mixture of the two with no residual sugar to influence the issue will have an intermediate specific gravity. In general, then, the winemaker can expect the specific gravity of a wine which is completely dry to be around 0.990-0.993. What is more, when the gravity of a fermenting must approaches this point, it is a sure indication that little sugar remains and fermentation is nearing completion.

The hydrometer can also be used to determine when fermentation has ceased even if all the sugar in the must has not been consumed by the yeast. In this instance, the final specific gravity will be higher than that of a dry wine due to the residual sugar. The hydrometer is still able to show when fermentation is complete under these circumstances because the gravity recorded will remain the same over a period of about 10-14 days. Yeast activity is then so slow that there is no point in prolonging matters and the wine should be siphoned off its sediment.

Yet another valuable service the hydrometer can perform is to indicate how well fermentation is proceeding. The rate at which the gravity is dropping is a direct measure of the rate of fermentation, so that the winemaker can assess the progress of a fermentation simply by measuring the gravity of the must at regular intervals and recording these readings. This technique is even more revealing if the results are plotted in the form of a graph.

It is not difficult to understand from these remarks why most experienced winemakers regard their hydrometer so highly and would not be without it. Few investments can offer so much in return! The hydrometer takes a great deal of the guesswork out of winemaking and is a tremendous help in the production of good quality wines. Its purchase should therefore rank very high on the list of priorities when buying the basic equipment needed for the wine cellar.

Gravity Tables

Specific Gravity	Gravity	Balling or Brix	Approx. Weight of Sugar gms/ litre	Approx. Weight of Sugar oz/Imp gal.	Potential Alcohol % by Vol.
1.000	0	0.0	0	0	0.0
1.005	5	1.7	4	½	0.1
1.010	10	3.0	17	3	0.8
1.015	15	4.3	30	5	1.6
1.020	20	5.5	44	7	2.4
1.025	25	6.8	57	9	3.2
1.030	30	8.0	70	11	3.9
1.035	35	9.2	83	13	4.7
1.040	40	10.4	97	15	5.5
1.045	45	11.6	110	17	6.2
1.050	50	12.8	123	19	7.0
1.055	55	14.0	136	21	7.6
1.060	60	15.2	149	24	8.4
1.065	65	16.4	163	26	9.1
1.070	70	17.6	176	28	9.9
1.075	75	18.7	189	30	10.7
1.080	80	19.8	202	32	11.4
1.085	85	20.9	215	34	12.2
1.090	90	22.0	228	36	12.9
1.095	95	23.1	242	38	13.7
1.100	100	24.2	255	40	14.5
1.105	105	25.3	268	43	15.2
1.110	110	26.4	282	45	16.0
1.115	115	27.5	295	47	16.7
1.120	120	28.5	308	49	17.4
1.125	125	29.6	321	51	18.2
1.130	130	30.6	335	53	18.9

Notes: The figures in this table make allowance for the effects of dissolved solids other than sugar. It has also been assumed that the bulk of the sugar in the must will be derived from natural sources.

Cleaning and Sterilizing

Cleanliness is said to be next to godliness and nowhere is this adage more true than in winemaking. Musts and wines are very rich media capable of supporting the growth of many bacteria and fungi which could quickly cause spoilage were they allowed to develop and multiply unchecked. It is therefore essential to take every precaution to exclude these undesirable micro-organisms as far as possible at all stages in the production of wine to ensure that it remains sound. Since a few will still inevitably gain access, it is equally as necessary to have some means of destroying these invaders or rendering them harmless before they can adversely affect the wine.

The first principle to follow in this fight against spoilage is to keep all musts and wines closely covered at all times with a cloth or a fermentation lock as recommended earlier. Some exposure obviously cannot be avoided, e.g. when transferring a must from the primary to the secondary fermentation vessel, but it should be kept to a minimum to reduce the risk of contamination by airborne or insect-borne spoilage organisms.

Secondly, every piece of equipment should be thoroughly washed and rinsed as soon as is conveniently possible after it has been used in case it is later overlooked and becomes an unsuspected breeding ground for inimical bacteria and fungi. Any spillages and splashes of wine should be mopped up immediately for the same reason.

In addition to this common sense approach of keeping everything clean, it is also a golden rule that equipment should always be sterilized before it comes into contact with a must or wine. This objective can best be achieved by washing or immersing each item in a sterilizing solution containing sulphur dioxide which can very easily be prepared from a substance properly identified as sodium metabisulphite but more commonly known just as sulphite by the winemaking community. Potassium metabisulphite may be employed instead of the sodium salt, but it is rather more expensive.

Some winemakers prefer to prepare this solution from a proprietary form of sulphite called Campden tablets, and this approach cannot really be faulted. On the other hand, experience has shown that it is much cheaper and more convenient to make it up by buying sulphite in bulk and dissolving the appropriate amount in water to produce a strong sterilizing solution.

A 10% stock sulphite solution is an excellent sterilizing agent which can easily be prepared by adding 4 ozs. (110 gms.) sodium metabisulphite to about 1½ pints (800 mls.) of warm water, stirring until it has completely dissolved and then adjusting its volume to 40 fl. ozs. (1 litre) with cold water. Great accuracy is not required here and the solution will keep for several months if it is stored in a tightly sealed bottle.

This solution should not be discarded after being employed to sterilize equipment but should be returned to the storage container for re-use. Some discolouration will inevitably occur as a result of repeated use, but the strength of the solution will scarcely be impaired if it is handled properly. To ensure that deterioration does not reduce its efficiency, however, a fresh stock solution should be made up every 2-3 months.

Equipment is by no means the only source of spoilage organisms. The ubiquitous fruit fly, which mysteriously appears from nowhere whenever the smell of wine pervades the air, frequently acts as a carrier of vinegar bacteria and their allies. Fungal spores and bacterial cells float freely around in the air and may inadvertently be incorporated into the must or wine. Some may even be intimately associated with the ingredients from which the wine is produced and thereby prove impossible to exclude. In other words, a wine may become contaminated with spoilage organisms either when the must is being prepared or at some later stage in its production, and it is important to realize that spoilage can come about in this way too.

To guard against such unfortunate accidents, the winemaker need merely add a little 10% stock sulphite solution to the must at the rate of ¼-½ fl. oz. per gallon (1-2 mls. per litre) some 18-24 hours before inoculating it with the yeast which will ferment it into wine. The reason for this delay is simply that the potency of the added sulphite diminishes appreciably with time. Thus, by introducing the yeast a day or so after the must has been sulphited, it is not exposed to the full effects of the sulphite as were any undesirable organisms already in the must.

The yeast is therefore able to grow and reproduce without hindrance because competing bacteria and fungi have either been killed or paralyzed by the sulphite and have not had time to recover from its impact. Occasional light sulphiting is also advisable while the young wine is clearing and maturing as insurance against infection, but this procedure will be more fully described in a later section.

Yeast

Wine is produced by a process known as fermentation during which yeast converts the sugar in the must into almost equal amounts of alcohol and carbon dioxide. Although most people are familiar with yeast, not many realize that it is a living organism properly classified as a plant. Yeast is in fact a simple type of fungus, and the Latin name of the family to which it belongs, *Saccharomyces,* which means sugar fungi, aptly reflects its rôle in life.

There are many different species of yeast, but very few of them are suitable for winemaking. Baker's yeast has traditionally been employed for making wine as well as for making dough rise and it undoubtedly is capable of producing good wine, but it certainly cannot be regarded as ideal for this purpose. Two of its major defects are the fluffy nature of the deposit formed during fermentation and the rapidity with which the dead yeast cells decompose and release off-flavours into the wine. Brewer's yeast is even worse in these respects and may in addition impart a beery flavour due to the hop residues it often contains.

At one time, the winemaker had little choice but to add baker's yeast to the must or follow the highly risky procedure of allowing a wild yeast to gain access to it, but this is no longer the case. Every store stocking winemaking supplies nowadays carries a large range of true wine yeasts, botanically identified as *Saccharomyces Ellipsoideus,* and they are so cheap that there is absolutely no reason for not using them from the beginning.

Some confusion may be felt at first when confronted by a host of different yeasts variously described as Bordeaux, Burgundy, Beaujolais, Montrachet, Champagne and so on. In reality, there is little to choose between most of these varieties, but to be sure that nothing goes amiss the winemaker is well advised to select what is called a general purpose yeast if the recipe fails to specify a particular type.

Wine yeasts come in several forms, the two most popular being the liquid culture and the sachet of dried granules. The liquid culture, which consists of dormant yeast cells suspended in a sterile nutrient solution, is inherently the better. On the other hand, its shelf life is limited and the yeast may prove difficult to reactivate if it has been stored for too long a time. Fortunately, dried yeasts are much purer, more reliable and better packaged than they were when they originally appeared on the market, so that the winemaker can now use them with every confidence.

It is perhaps pertinent to mention here that a wine yeast bearing the name of a famous wine-growing district does not automatically possess the ability to confer the characteristics of the wine produced there on any must inoculated with it. All it actually means is that this particular yeast has been isolated from the bloom found on grapes growing in that region (or from some other source there), subjected to extensive laboratory evaluations and finally released as a pure culture typical of the yeast indigenous to that part of the world.

In other words, the so-called named wine yeasts possess no magical properties capable of converting any must into the type of wine with which they have been associated as a result of common origin, even though they are usually excellent yeasts for most winemaking purposes. As may be expected, there are a few exceptions to this rule, notably sherry and champagne yeasts, but for the most part they can be ignored by the less experienced winemaker mainly interested in producing pleasantly enjoyable wines for serving at the table or on social occasions.

Yeast Starters

It is commonly recommended that dried yeasts and certain liquid cultures be added directly to the must to start it fermenting, but this practice leaves a great deal to be desired. A far better procedure is to activate and propagate the yeast by preparing what is called a starter. Its purpose is to ensure that the yeast is in good condition and in a state of active fermentation when it is introduced into the must. A starter also serves the very important function of increasing the amount of yeast to many times that supplied in the original culture. Thus, following its incorporation, the must will begin to ferment much sooner than would have been the case had the yeast been introduced directly.

The wise winemaker always activates the yeast in this way a day or two before preparing the must to be certain that the starter is ready for use immediately it is required. Proprietary yeast starter mixes, which are generally based on dried malt extract and come with detailed instructions, are usually quite good and reliable. Alternatively, the following simple technique has been found to work extremely well and has the advantage of needing no specialized ingredients.

Purchase a small 6-7 fl. oz. (175-200 mls.) can of frozen orange concentrate from a local supermarket and dilute it with water according to the directions on the can. Take about 5 fl. ozs. (150 mls) of this juice, add 1 tbsp. sugar and stir until it has dissolved. Pour this sweetened juice into a small saucepan and bring it to the boil. Hold the juice at the boiling point for about a minute to sterilize it, then cool it rapidly under the tap to a temperature of 85°F (30°C) or less.

Sterilize an ordinary wine bottle with 10% stock sulphite solution, making sure that it reaches every part of the interior surface. Return the sulphite solution to its storage container, then rinse the wine bottle once or twice with a little cold boiled water to flush out residual sulphite. Add the sterilized orange juice to this freshly sterilized bottle and pour in the yeast. Plug the neck of the bottle firmly with a wad of cotton wool and stand it in a warm place.

A fresh yeast culture will set this starter bottle fermenting within 24 hours, but it may take several days before any signs of fermentation become apparent when an older or less viable culture is employed. The starter is ready for use as soon as it begins to ferment and will provide enough yeast for 1-2 gallons (5-10 litres) of must. For larger quantities of must, the amount of starter required will be 3-5% of the total volume contemplated and as many starter bottles as will be needed may be prepared according to the preceding directions.

Yeast Nutrients

Like many other living organisms, yeast needs a number of trace elements and vitamins in addition to its principal food in order to remain in sound and healthy condition. Most of these substances are already present naturally in a well balanced must in amounts adequate to ensure the growth and development of a flourishing yeast colony, but sometimes a shortage does occur. Since any lack of nutrients can seriously reduce the rate and vigour of fermentation or even cause it to stick, it is wise to add some routinely to every must as an insurance against any problems arising on this account.

The major elements essential for a strong fermentation include nitrogen and phosphorus, and both can conveniently be provided by adding ammonium phosphate at the rate of about ½ tsp. per gallon (5 litres). Since other key elements may also be in short supply, however, it is perhaps even better to add 1 tsp. per gallon (5 litres) of a proprietary nutrient mixture which is a blend of mineral substances important for the continued wellbeing of the yeast. Many winemakers in fact make doubly sure that the yeast is well nourished by adding ¼ tsp. per gallon (5 litres) of a proprietary yeast energizer over and above the standard nutrients in order to furnish vitamins and allied growth-regulating factors, and this practice has much to commend it.

Fermentation

Yeast changes a must into wine by converting the sugar it contains into almost equal weights of alcohol and carbon dioxide. The latter, being a gas, rises through the fermenting must as myriads of tiny bubbles which burst at the surface to release the carbon dioxide which finally escapes to the air through the fermentation lock. The alcohol, of course, remains behind to give the wine its stimulating and mellowing influence.

Since the amount of alcohol generated during fermentation obviously depends upon the weight of the sugar consumed by the yeast, it should therefore be possible to regulate the alcoholic strength of a wine by controlling the quantity of sugar initially present in the must. This idea is basically correct.

For table wines, the winemaker should aim for a must with 2 lbs. sugar per gallon (200 gms. per litre) in order to obtain an alcohol content around 12% by volume which is a fairly standard table wine strength. The recipes in this book have in fact been designed to produce wines of this type, i.e. the total natural and added sugar in the must comes close to the above figure.

It should also be realized that there is an upper limit to the amount of alcohol which can be obtained by fermentation. Alcohol is really a by-product of yeast activity and is actually poisonous to yeast when its concentration becomes too high. Thus, for most practical purposes, fermentation cannot be guaranteed to yield more than about 16% alcohol by volume even though it can on occasion achieve 18-20% or more. Adding extra sugar to the must consequently may not only fail to result in a high alcoholic strength but may also leave the wine sweet rather than dry if the yeast has been unable to handle all this sugar.

Fermentation may be divided into several phases of which the primary and secondary fermentations are perhaps the most notable. Although these two stages are rather arbitrarily defined and tend to merge imperceptibly from one into the other, there are good reasons for distinguishing between them.

The action starts with the primary fermentation which is a time of great yeast activity. Copious volumes of carbon dioxide are given off and the must usually froths and foams quite spectacularly. Several inches or more of foam commonly accumulate on the surface of the must at this time and there is a distinct tendency for it to overflow its container. This is why fermentation is started in a wide-mouthed primary fermentation vessel with a capacity considerably larger than the volume of the must, for such a container can cope with a frothy, foaming must without spillage and is easy to clean after this initial tumultuous stage is over.

The primary fermentation will normally continue for some 5-8 days, but sooner or later its vigour will begin to abate, the frothing and foaming will die down and the fermentation will proceed quietly but steadily. Once this point is reached, the must has entered the secondary phase of fermentation. It can now be transferred to the secondary fermentation vessel under an air lock with little risk of the contents overflowing, and left there to ferment to dryness.

Fermentation should ideally be conducted at a temperature of 65-70°F (18-21°C) which may be possible in a cool cellar during the winter but is otherwise likely to prove difficult to achieve in the absence of air conditioning. Normal summer temperatures and central heating conspire to make a temperature range of 70-80°F (21-27°C) more probable, which is acceptable although fermentation will tend to be more rapid and vigorous under these conditions. The winemaker should always try not to exceed 80°F (27°C), for yeast becomes weakened and spoilage organisms are encouraged by temperatures much above this reading.

Acid Balance

A properly balanced acidity is essential for the production of pleasant, palatable wine. Too much acid means that the wine will taste tart or sour in the sense that lemon juice is said to be sour, sometimes to the extent that it becomes undrinkable. Too little acid has just the opposite effect, for then the wine will appear insipid, lifeless and altogether lacking in appeal. Moreover, if fermentation is allowed to proceed in a must virtually devoid of acid, the result is a "wine" which tastes like cough medicine.

The amount of acid in a must or wine can be measured with the aid of a fairly simple acid testing kit. The result will be expressed as parts per thousand (ppt) of tartaric acid, and for most purposes a wine should contain between 4.5 ppt and 7.0 ppt of acid on this scale. In practice, around 5.0-5.5 ppt will be found to be a good average level at which to aim.

If more than 7.0 ppt acid are present it may be suitably reduced simply by diluting the must appropriately with water. Should the acidity lie below 4.5 ppt, some acid should be added, preferably in the form of an acid blend consisting of a mixture of citric acid, malic acid and tartaric acid in equal proportions. In this connection, it should be remembered that the addition of ¼ oz. of this acid blend per gallon (1½ gms. per litre) will increase the acidity of the must by approximately 1.5 ppt.

Many less experienced winemakers find the subject of acidity complex and confusing. Under these circumstances, the best course of action is to ignore it altogether and select only properly designed recipes which ensure that the must starts off with a balanced acidity. Since the recipes in this book all come into this category, the winemaker may follow them with every confidence without having to check the acidity of the must.

Tannin

All wines need tannin to give them a pleasant astringency. If no tannin is present, the wine will taste flat and lack character in much the same way as it does when it contains insufficient acid. An excess of tannin is equally as bad, for then the wine will be rough and harsh on the palate with a tendency to pucker up the mouth just as sloes do. Indeed, sloes have this effect because they are richly endowed with tannin.

Red wines generally contain more tannin than white or rosé wines which is one reason why they often appear drier to the palate. Since tannin helps a wine to clear by combining with and removing proteins and allied constituents which can cause hazes, the larger amounts associated with red wines is an important reason why these wines normally fall bright and clear more quickly and easily than white wines.

Tannin is found in the skins and seeds of most fruits and is especially abundant in red fruits where it accompanies the colouring matter. The tannic acid of commerce is actually extracted from acorns and comes as

Some standard wine bottles. From left to right: red Bordeaux, white Bordeaux, red Burgundy, white Burgundy, Champagne, Rhine or Moselle.

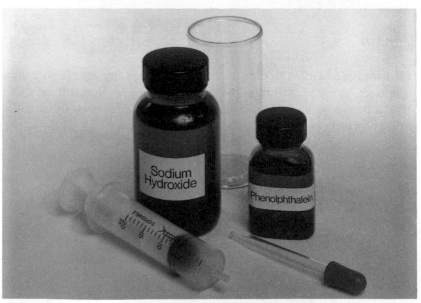

Equipment and standard solutions for acid testing.

a light, fluffy powder which varies in colour from a pale tan to a definite brown. Grape tannin is obtained from grape seeds and is usually darker than tannic acid. Although it would be reasonable to assume that grape tannin is preferable for winemaking purposes, experience has in fact shown that tannic acid is equally as good, so that either may be used whenever a recipe calls for tannin.

Unlike acidity which can be measured fairly simply, the tannin content of a must or wine can be determined only by a complex and difficult analytical procedure. The winemaker must therefore rely upon past experience to know when to add tannin or again follow reliable recipes which indicate how much tannin is required, as do those in this book.

Racking and Clarification

Once fermentation has come to an end, suspended yeast cells and other insoluble matter begin to sink to the bottom of the secondary fermentation vessel to form a sediment called the lees. Wine must not be left standing on its lees for too long, otherwise it is apt to acquire musty off-flavours due to the decomposition of dead yeast cells and other debris comprising the deposit. It is therefore decanted or siphoned off the lees about a week or so after fermentation has ceased, and this process is known as racking.

As the suspended materials slowly settle out, the wine gradually becomes clearer. Periodic racking stimulates clarification, presumably as a result of the agitation and aeration the wine receives at this time, but excessive splashing should be avoided in case the wine absorbs too much oxygen from the air and becomes over-oxidized. The first racking generally takes place some 7-10 days following the termination of the fermentation, the delay serving to allow many of the coarser particles held in suspension to gather in the lees.

The timing of the second racking is more difficult to determine. Should a fairly thick deposit accumulate a few weeks after the first racking, it is best removed as soon as it is noticed to reduce the risk of off-flavours developing. Otherwise, the wine will be due for its second racking some 2-3 months after the first. A third racking will usually be needed in another 3 months to effect complete clarification, by which time the wine will be about 6 months old and may already be pleasantly drinkable.

In practice, wine is racked by siphoning it from one container to another with the aid of a piece of flexible plastic tubing 5-6 feet (2 metres) long with a bore of about ⅜ths of an inch (9 mm). To avoid sucking up sediment from the bottom of the secondary fermentation vessel during this operation, most winemakers attach a J-tube to the end of the siphon inserted into the latter container.

A J-tube is simply a length of glass or rigid plastic tubing turned up at one end just enough for it to stand clear of the lees. Wine enters this J-tube from the direction of the surface rather than from the direction of the lees, so that there is much less danger of disturbing the deposit and drawing it into the stream of wine.

It is advisable to guard the wine against possible infection and the effects of oxidation when it is racked by adding a little 10% stock sulphite solution at the rate of ¼-½ fl. oz. per gallon (1-2 mls. per litre). For the best results, the sulphite solution should be poured into the receiving vessel prior to starting racking operations so that the wine enjoys the fullest possible protection from the outset. Although light sulphiting can be carried out each time a wine is racked, a rather better practice is to add the above dose of sulphite solution after the first racking, none after the second and half that amount at the third.

Sometimes a wine will refuse to clear and will still be hazy by the time the third racking falls due, even though it has apparently been treated no differently from any other batch produced previously. The reason for this abnormal behaviour may possibly be traced to the presence of pectin in the wine. Pectin is the substance which causes jam to set, and there it fulfils a valuable function. Pectin in wine is quite another matter, for it prevents the tiny particles responsible for hazes from settling so that a permanently cloudy wine is obtained.

Fortunately, this problem is very easily removed by adding to the must a special enzyme preparation such as Pectinol which destroys pectin. If all the pectin is disposed of prior to and during fermentation, hazes stabilized by pectin simply cannot form. It is therefore worth incorporating a little pectic enzyme into every must as a matter of course to avoid encountering difficulties of this nature, especially as the amount required is only ¼-½ tsp. per gallon (5 litres).

The only precaution to observe is not to add the pectic enzyme to a hot must, for it is itself destroyed by exposure to too high a temperature. A good rule of thumb here is to introduce the pectic enzyme with the yeast starter since conditions suitable for inoculating the must with the yeast will also be ideal for the enzyme.

A haze due to pectin is very easy to detect in a wine. A small sample of the wine, say 1 fl. oz. (25 mls.), is simply mixed with 3-4 volumes of methyl hydrate (obtainable from any chemist). If pectin is present, it will come out of solution in the form of gelatinous clots and strings. The winemaker then knows for certain that pectin is responsible and should add pectic enzyme to the wine at the rate recommended earlier, for it is also effective when fermentation is over.

Should this test prove negative, the winemaker can only conclude that the wine has failed to clear for some other more obscure reason. Under these circumstances, the best approach is to fine the wine, i.e. to treat it with something which will promote clarification. Although there are many good fining agents, it is perhaps preferable for the less experienced winemaker to employ a reliable proprietary preparation for this purpose. Full instructions for the use of these products are normally provided with them and they usually work well. Following fining, the clarified wine should be racked off the sediment which forms, just as if it had cleared naturally.

Maturing

A new wine sampled at the first racking almost invariably looks and tastes rather uninviting. It is then usually quite cloudy with a distinctly yeasty character and a harsh, often unpleasant taste. Several months later, the wine will have cleared to brilliance and will possess an attractive bouquet and flavour. These rather astounding changes do not come about suddenly but take place gradually as the wine grows older, and this process of progressive improvement with time is called maturing.

It sometimes takes many years for a wine to mature to its peak of perfection, e.g. the great clarets and red Burgundies of commerce, but other less pretentious wines, which in reality represent the bulk of the world's production, are ready for drinking at a much younger age. The recipes in this book certainly come under this heading, for they are designed to produce wines which will be pleasantly drinkable when they are only a few months old.

A wine improves with time due partly to the deposition of suspended matter which commonly imparts a harsh or bitter taste but mainly to the

25

occurrence of complicated chemical interactions between its various alcohols, sugars, acids, salts and other constituents. The complexity of the chemical changes which take place in a maturing wine is such that they have still been explained only in relatively general terms. This aspect of maturing is therefore far beyond the scope of this book.

The important point to remember is that a maturing wine, particularly a red wine, requires a certain amount of oxygen to develop properly. Since glass is impermeable to air, wine stored in glass containers depends upon the aeration it receives during racking for the supply of oxygen it needs. On the other hand, too much oxygen is even worse than too little because the wine will become flat and lifeless due to over-oxidation and may not recover from this condition, especially if it is a light delicate white wine. Violent splashing must therefore be avoided and the wine should be racked into a pre-sulphited container as recommended in the previous section.

Maturing wine should ideally be stored in a dark cool place whose temperature remains at a constant 55-60°F (13-16°C) all year round. Some winemakers are lucky enough to possess a cool cellar which acts as an excellent wine storage area, but such happy situations are all too rare.

Since wine deteriorates on exposure to bright light for any length of time, there is no escaping the necessity to store it in a dark location such as a corner of the attic or a convenient large cupboard. Temperature is rather less critical in that a wine will not suffer unduly if it is kept in warmer surroundings than the ideal 55-60°F (13-16°C) provided it remains constant for much of the year, e.g. at about 75°F (24°C) all summer and around 65°F (18°C) during the winter. What must be avoided are rapid fluctuations in temperature, say from 75°F (24°C) during the day to 65°F (18°C) at night every 24 hours, for then the wine will be adversely affected.

Although it is impossible to specify in advance just how long it will take a wine to reach complete maturity, few are really ready to drink before they are 4-6 months old. Many wines benefit from considerably longer maturing, but care has been taken to ensure that most of the wines produced from recipes in this book will be drinkable at a fairly young age. On the other hand, many of these wines will continue to improve for some time longer and could advantageously be matured for a few more months after they are bottled. It all depends how much patience (and wine) the winemaker happens to have!

Spoilage

The spectre of spoilage is something that no winemaker likes even to think about, and modern methods of winemaking have done much to eliminate the risk of losing wine as a result of microbial infection. Unfortunately, the occasional batch of wine may become contaminated by inimical micro-organisms and then it is essential to know what steps to take to save the wine if this is at all possible.

Perhaps the most common, and at the same time one of the most catastrophic, infections to afflict a wine is for it to start to go sour and turn into vinegar. This disaster can at once be recognized by the strong vinegary smell and taste which develop in the wine, and the invading organisms must be eradicated with all possible speed if the winemaker wants to hold any hopes of saving the wine from their depredations.

Acetification, as this form of spoilage is called, is caused by various species of vinegar bacteria which may be introduced in a number of ways. The ingredients of the must are one potential source, which is why a must prepared from ingredients likely to act as carriers of spoilage organisms should always be sterilized prior to fermentation. Airborne bacterial cells may also be responsible, but by far the most likely culprit is the ubiquitous fruit fly which is irresistibly attracted by fermenting musts and usually brings with it a surprising selection of vinegar bacteria.

Since vinegar bacteria are quite sensitive to sulphite, an elementary programme of hygiene coupled with regular sulphiting will normally obviate the danger of acetification. If a wine does start turning to vinegar because these precautions have not been properly observed, it is probably not worth the effort of trying to save it.

The powerful vinegary bouquet and flavour which develops within a short time of the infection becoming established leaves the winemaker very little leeway to counter it effectively. Sulphite will kill the bacteria responsible and prevent the wine from deteriorating further, but it will not remove the vinegary character which has already manifested itself.

The simplest approach under these circumstances is therefore to segregate any wine which begins to acetify and leave it to one side until it has gone completely to vinegar. It may then be employed in the kitchen for cooking, on salads and so on as wine vinegar, which is an expensive commodity to buy.

Sometimes a wine will acquire a peculiar off-flavour so that it tastes cheesy, mousy or simply bitter. The bouquet too may become rather acrid and gas bubbles may form in the wine. More than one of these symptoms may be observed at the same time, and they are characteristic of various wine diseases such as tourne, amertume and the like which are all caused by one species or another of a large group of micro-organisms classified as the lactic acid bacteria.

Since spoilage due to lactic acid bacteria takes time to develop, their presence in a wine is not immediately apparent and it is usually beyond redemption before the winemaker really comprehends what is happening. Even when it does become obvious that something is wrong with the wine, some winemakers do not realize that it is suffering from a bacterial infection and often ascribe the incidence of these off-flavours to poor storage, improper racking or some other error in technique. Lactic acid bacteria are insidious in their attack and as a result are the unsuspected cause of much more wine being lost than is generally appreciated.

Most species of lactic acid bacteria are quickly killed by sulphite so that once again regular sulphiting along the lines recommended earlier will usually prevent them from becoming established in a wine. Prevention is the keynote here, for little can be done once lactic acid bacteria have spoiled its bouquet and flavour.

The same applies to another common affliction called flowers of wine. A whitish film gradually grows on the surface of the wine, and if nothing is done about it the wine eventually becomes flat and lifeless. Flowers of wine is rather more resistant to sulphite than are acetic and lactic acid bacteria, but its growth will be greatly discourged if not completely terminated by ensuring that the wine is adequately sulphited at all times.

It is clear from these remarks that the key to keeping wine sound and free from marauding micro-organisms is simply to ensure that everything in the wine cellar is always clean and sterile so that no potential sources of infection remain. In addition, the wine itself should be regularly sulphited in order to inhibit any bacteria or fungi which do gain access from growing and developing to the detriment of the wine. The winemaker who follows these practices is unlikely to be troubled by batches of spoiled wine.

CHAPTER 2

Grape Concentrate

Grape concentrate was hailed as the answer to every winemaker's prayer when it first appeared on the winemaking scene here in Britain many years ago. In a country where grapes can only be grown successfully under glass except in a few climatically favoured areas, grape concentrate certainly offered most winemakers an opportunity to produce wine from pure grape juice for the first time. Moreover, the reputation of the grape as the winemaking fruit *par excellence* also led many prominent winemakers to believe that grape concentrate would provide an easy and straightforward route to the production of superior wines.

Much apprehension was nevertheless felt in certain quarters that the winemaking movement as a whole stood to lose more than it was going to gain as a result of the introduction of grape concentrate. If wine was so simple to make from concentrate and would really attain such a high standard of quality as was being implied, then it would not be worth the time and effort to produce it from other more prosaic, indigenous ingredients, or so it was thought. Basic winemaking skills would therefore be lost, and with their demise quality would eventually suffer.

As it has turned out, neither of these predictions has come to pass. Enormous amounts of grape concentrate are nowadays being sold for winemaking purposes and very pleasant wine it makes too, but other ingredients have certainly not been superseded because they have also been found capable of producing excellent wine in their own right. In addition, it was discovered in these early days that grape concentrate did not always yield the superior wine which had been so eagerly and confidently anticipated but sometimes produced wine of very average quality.

In hindsight, the reasons why some concentrates did not initially live up to their billing are fairly easy to assess. Concentrate quality ranks high on the list in this connection. Certain of the grape concentrates which first appeared on the market were not manufactured for winemaking purposes at all but were intended for other applications where poor colour and some degree of caramelization of the sugars were quite acceptable.

Needless to say, these concentrates did not produce particularly good wine, but their sales continued to grow because winemakers were always willing to try a few batches of grape wine. As a result it was some years before these suppliers of grape concentrate began to realize that winemakers really did require superior grades of concentrate and were willing to pay premium prices for them.

As demand for grape concentrate increased, more and more importance became attached to the quality of the wine which could be produced from it so that progressively better concentrates steadily started to appear. This continuing emphasis on quality has resulted in a similar improvement in the wine produced from it. Although the original idea that such wines would vie with the best of their commercial counterparts may now be regarded as overly optimistic, they certainly compare favourably with many which are now commanding high prices everywhere. There can certainly be little doubt the concentrate offers a very easy way to make pleasant wines eminently suitable for daily household needs.

How, then, is grape concentrate actually produced? The process most commonly employed at the present time is called vacuum distillation and is relatively simple to follow.

Freshly picked grapes are first of all fed into a piece of equipment called a crusher-stemmer that simultaneously crushes the berries and separates them from the stems, which are discarded. The resultant mixture of juice and pulp is then treated with sulphur dioxide to kill or paralyze unwanted micro-organisms and a pectin-destroying enzyme is introduced to degrade the pectins and facilitate further processing.

The next stage in the proceedings depends upon the type of grape being handled and whether it is intended for conversion into white or red concentrate. Grapes destined for the production of white concentrate are simply pressed and the juice pumped into a holding tank where it is cooled and stored for some time to allow the coarser pieces of pulp carried over from the crusher to settle out. The partially clarified juice is then racked off the pulp deposit. This procedure may be repeated several times to remove the bulk of the suspended pulp particles and reduce the load on the system of filters or centrifuges which take out the remaining insoluble solids to yield a brilliantly clear juice suitable for concentration.

Red grapes follow a somewhat different path because colour must usually be extracted from their skins before the juice can be separated from the pulp. Since the colouring matter in red grapes is insoluble in the cold juice and pulp fermentation techniques whereby the alcohol generated by the fermentation bleaches the colour from the skins cannot be employed, the production of red grape concentrate obviously presents more of a problem than might at first be expected.

Fortunately, the substances responsible for the colour of red grapes will dissolve in the hot juice, so that concentrate manufacturers merely heat the mixture of juice and pulp coming from the crushers to a temperature of about 140°F (60°C) for some hours until enough colour has been extracted from the skins to give a dark red juice. The latter is then cooled, pressed, settled, racked, centrifuged and filtered to render it brilliantly clear exactly as already described for juices intended for the production of white grape concentrates.

This extra step of colour extraction is in fact the only significant difference between the methods used to prepare red and white grape concentrates. The actual process of concentration is carried out in the same way regardless of the colour of the incoming juice. At present, concentration is usually effected by vacuum distillation because equipment suitable for this purpose was already in operation in many grape growing areas, but alternative techniques such as freeze-drying are also being evaluated. The majority of these vacuum distillation facilities were actually constructed for concentrating orange juice but they turned their attention to the concentration of grape juice when the demand for this product increased dramatically due its rising popularity among winemakers.

Although the quality of grape concentrate depends to some degree upon the variety of grape from which it is derived, it is even more strongly influenced by the skill with which concentration is carried out. Great care and attention are required at all stages in the concentration process to avoid contamination by undesirable micro-organisms, excessive oxidation, caramelization of the sugars and similar disasters.

When the concentrate is produced by vacuum distillation, as is generally the case at the present time, very close control must be exercised over this particularly crucial stage in its manufacture in order to ensure that a superior concentrate is obtained.

The principle of vacuum distillation is that water boils at a lower temperature when the pressure is reduced, a fact which will be familiar to anyone who has experienced living at a high altitude, e.g. in Mexico City. Thus, by placing grape juice under a partial vacuum, the water it contains can be induced to boil considerably below its normal boiling-point of 212°F (100°C). The actual temperature at which it does boil depends mainly upon how powerful a vacuum can be pulled above the juice, but in practice it is normally strong enough to bring the boiling-point well below 100°F (38°C).

The reason why grape juice must be concentrated under vacuum is that the sugars in it degrade and caramelize when exposed for any length of time to the temperatures at which the juice boils under atmospheric pressure. Concentrates prepared in this latter fashion, such as the *arropes* of Spain, are useful for sweetening and darkening the colour of sherries and similar wines, but they are so deeply coloured and strongly flavoured that they themselves make quite undrinkable wine if they are simply reconstituted with water and fermented in the normal manner.

These undesirable changes do not occur to any significant extent when concentration is accomplished by a properly conducted process of vacuum distillation because the temperature then never rises to the point at which the sugars in the juice undergo decomposition. Such concentrates can therefore be diluted back to their original volume with water and fermented into pleasantly drinkable wines.

It is nevertheless interesting to note that wines produced in this manner from concentrates are not quite the same as those made from the grapes as they come from the vine. Some of these differences are probably due to the vacuum distillation technique used to manufacture the concentrate. For example, even the comparatively low temperatures at which the water is evaporated may irreversibly change or even destroy thermally sensitive constituents of the juice, such as labile enzymes and proteins, without otherwise affecting the concentrate. Since these substances could well play some rôle during fermentation or, more likely, in the highly complex sequence of events involved in maturing, their loss could well account for some of the differences which have been observed.

Other constituents of the juice are also evaporated and removed along with the water during concentration by vacuum distillation. Many of these components are more volatile than water and hence are more easily abstracted from the juice, so that none may remain in the concentrate prepared from it.

At one time, no attempt was made to recover these volatile constituents and return them to the concentrate with the result that the bouquet of the wine produced from it was rather faint and unattractive. Nowadays, their importance to the bouquet of the wine is recognized and most concentrate manufacturers take pains to separate them from the water simultaneously evaporated from the juice. This "bouquet fraction" is then blended back into the concentrate to ensure that the wine made from it will possess a fine bouquet.

Red wines produced from concentrate are usually less astringent than red wines produced directly from grapes. This difference can almost certainly be ascribed to the way in which the colour is extracted from the skins in the two cases. The colour of red grape concentrate is obtained by heating the mixture of juice and pulp emerging from the crushers to an elevated temperature for some time, whereas the colour of red wines is abstracted from the skins by fermenting them in contact with the juice until the alcohol generated by the fermentation has leached out enough of their colour to give a dark red must.

The point to bear in mind is that the alcohol formed during the period of pulp fermentation extracts not only colouring matter but also considerable amounts of tannins and related substances which contribute to the flavour and astringency of the wine. By way of contrast, heating the mass of juice and pulp seems to favour the removal of colour rather than tannins and the like from the skins because comparatively little of these latter constituents can be found in the juice unless heating is continued until it becomes very dark in colour. It is also notable that these intensely coloured red concentrates tend to produce wines which are more astringent than those derived from concentrates less well endowed with colour and so, presumably, also containing less tannins and allied components of the skins.

This lower tannin content of red wines produced from concentrate has the advantage that they are ready to drink at a relatively tender age. Wines rich in tannin take years to lose their harshness and mellow, which is why red wines made from fresh grapes are undrinkable when young and do not become fully mature until they have been aged in a cask or bottle for long periods of time. The winemaker is therefore able to enjoy both red and white wines within a few months of making them from concentrate instead of having to wait for years as would be the case were they produced from fresh grapes.

Practical Aspects

Grape concentrate makes a tremendously important contribution to winemaking in a variety of ways. To begin with, it is hard to imagine anything simpler than making wine from concentrate. It need only be diluted with water and the recommended amounts of sugar, nutrients, acids and so on dissolved in it to give a must ready for fermentation. Some yeast starter is then added and the must is allowed to ferment to dryness under an air lock.

Clear wine is usually obtained after the second or third racking by which time it will probably be pleasantly drinkable, but it is better to keep the new wine for 3-6 months after fermentation has ceased before trying it. Since wines produced from concentrate are designed to be drunk while they are young, lengthy maturing is not necessary so that such wines are ready for the table when they are 6-12 months old.

Concentrate is clearly ideal for the beginner just starting to make wine. Little can go wrong during the preparation of the must and the chances of contamination by inimical micro-organisms are minimal. At the same time, the beginner gains valuable experience and confidence in carrying out unfamiliar tasks, e.g. using a hydrometer and interpreting its readings.

Fermentation too is hardly likely to falter due to a shortage of nutrients because it is taking place in what is essentially pure grape juice, a medium well endowed with an ample supply of natural nutrients which most winemakers augment by adding more when the concentrate is reconstituted with water. Finally, and perhaps most important of all, wine made from grape concentrate normally clears rapidly and does not require years of maturing before it can be properly enjoyed. Instead, it is eminently drinkable within a matter of months, a prospect which the thirsty beginner with no stocks of wine to tap finds extremely attractive.

These remarks indicate but a few of the many good reasons why beginners are well advised to start their winemaking career with grape concentrate. They also reveal that lack of space need not be a deterrent to making wine at home, even when home may lie within the confines of a small apartment. Space can always be found for a 5-6 gallon jar or demi-john, a few gallon jars and a dozen or two bottles in even the most cramped conditions, and little else in the way of equipment is required to make a batch of wine from grape concentrate.

Since the wine is ready to drink at an age of only a few months, little storage space is necessary so that it is perfectly feasible to start a new batch fermenting every couple of weeks, which adds up to a grand total of about 25 gallons (100 litres) per year. Grape concentrate therefore offers the apartment dweller the opportunity to enjoy a bottle of sound, pleasant wine every day without having to take over more than a nominal amount of the living area with bottles of maturing wine in order to do so.

Concentrate has the further advantage of being readily available at all times of the year. Winemaking can therefore be a year-round pursuit rather than a seasonal flurry of anxious activity in the autumn as is the case when fresh grapes and other fruits are used. Smaller batches of wine can be made throughout the year rather than a single large quantity all at the one time even though the total annual production may remain the same. Much more variety is possible with concentrate too.

Another far-reaching and valuable attribute of grape concentrate is what it can do to improve the quality of wines prepared primarily from other ingredients. Until the advent of grape concentrate, raisins were widely included at the rate of 1-2 lbs. per gallon (100-200 gms. per litre) to add character and vinosity to wines which would otherwise lack these essential commodities. Nowadays, raisins have been largely superseded in this rôle by grape concentrate which can work wonders in terms of quality when incorporated to the extent of ½ -1 pint per gallon of must (75-125 mls. per litre).

Although the addition of grape concentrate is by no means necessary when good wine can be expected from an undiluted or lightly diluted fruit juice, e.g. apple and pear juices, even then it can often be advantageously employed instead of granulated sugar to increase the natural sugar content of these juices to a level acceptable for table wine production. This technique is particularly useful when a fuller-bodied and altogether richer wine is desired.

On the other hand, should extensive dilution with water be required to reduce acidity or to mute a powerful ingredient flavour, grape concentrate offers one of the best ways to replace at least some of the body and much of the vinous quality thereby lost. Its inclusion under these circumstances is consequently almost mandatory if quality is a major consideration, and it is for this reason that concentrate so frequently figures prominently in recipes designed to produce superior wines.

Grape concentrates can nowadays be obtained from almost every important grape growing region in the world, but the chief sources of supply at the moment are Spain, Italy, France, Cyprus and Austria which export their concentrates to Britain and elsewhere under a large variety of different brand names. Naturally enough, every winemaker wants to know which of these many concentrates is the best, but a thorough evaluation of numerous widely stocked types failed to reveal any especially notable for their quality in comparison with the others. A few were found to be somewhat sub-standard, but there was surprisingly little to choose between the remainder whatever their origins.

How, then, can the winemaker assess the potential of a newly discovered type of grape concentrate? The only sure way of doing so is to buy some and try it on a small scale, but certain other criteria can often provide a useful guide in this respect rather more quickly. For example, the colour of the juice obtained after reconstituting the concentrate with 3-5 volumes of water gives a good indication of the care with which the concentrate was produced and stored. Thus, the juice prepared from red concentrate should be dark red or purplish-red in colour and free from brownish tints which suggest that excessive oxidation or even some caramelization has occurred. Similarly, the juice derived from white concentrate should be pale yellow or, at the worst, light amber in colour otherwise the wine will look unattractive and is apt to possess a poor flavour which can again be ascribed to over-oxidation or caramelization.

Clarity too is important. A concentrate which yields a cloudy juice on dilution with water is at once suspect because wine made from it usually proves difficult to clear unless the haze is due to suspended crystals of cream of tartar. Since many concentrates do contain a granular deposit of cream of tartar, it is fortunate that the crystals settle out within a few hours to leave a brilliantly clear juice. The winemaker should therefore experience no trouble in deciding if tartrate is the culprit when a cloudy juice is encountered.

Close attention should also be paid to the acid content of the concentrate which ideally should be about 25-30 ppt prior to dilution.

To begin with, the grapes from which concentrate is produced often come from areas where an abundance of sun and heat favours the development of a high sugar content and a low acidity. Again, some of the acid in the original grape juice is precipitated during the concentration process as cream of tartar which may be removed and discarded by the manufacturer but which in any case does not redissolve readily when the concentrate is reconstituted with water. As a result, concentrates tend to lack acid and any such deficiency must be made good prior to fermentation or the wine will taste flat and insipid. A mixture consisting of equal weights of citric, malic and tartaric acids should be used for this purpose.

The final feature to look at is the gravity of the concentrate. Many manufacturers aim for a finished gravity in the region of 330-340, which represents about a fourfold degree of concentration, because further concentration beyond this point becomes progressively more difficult to control without adversely affecting the quality of the concentrate and causes the precipitation of large amounts of cream of tartar. With modern equipment, however, it is perfectly feasible to achieve a gravity of 400 or more, although there is then the danger of losing too much acid in the form of cream of tartar unless precautions are taken to prevent its depositing. Concentrates may therefore vary in gravity from 330 or slightly lower to about 400, and it is notable that the higher gravity concentrates come mainly from Spain where some of the most sophisticated concentration plants in the world are located.

High gravity concentrates have the advantage that they often cost about the same as their lower gravity counterparts but make cheaper wine because a greater degree of dilution is required to reconstitute them as juice. At one time, this advantage was largely offset by their poorer quality due to the increased degradation and caramelization of the sugars which usually accompanied attempts to produce high gravity concentrates, but the advent of modern vacuum distillation techniques seems largely to have overcome these problems. The winemaker should nevertheless ascertain that this is indeed the case for any new brand of high gravity concentrate by making a small trial batch of wine from it for evaluation purposes. Indeed, it is wise to adopt this approach every time a new type of concentrate is encountered, whatever its gravity, to avoid expensive disappointments.

Experience has shown that both the cost and the quality of the wine produced from grape concentrates normally benefit if slightly more water than is needed to reduce their sugar content to its original level is added. The concentrate should in fact be diluted to a gravity of about 65-70 with 4-5 volumes of water and then readjusted to a gravity of approximately 85-90 with sugar or honey at the rate of roughly ½ lb. per gallon (50 gms. per litre) of diluted concentrate. At this point, its acidity should be checked and increased to 4.0-5.5 ppt. with a mixture consisting of equal amounts of citric, malic and tartaric acids if a deficiency is detected. All that then remains is to add the nutrients and the must is ready for inoculation with the yeast starter.

Although more extensive dilution is frequently suggested as a means of producing what have been termed light wines, it is really false economy to try to stretch a single gallon (5 litres) of concentrate into eight or more gllons (35 or more litres) of wine. Such wines typically turn out to have very little body and lack colour and flavour, so that the beginner is well advised to avoid the temptation to cut costs by making so-called light wines which even the untrained palate will recognise as inferior in quality.

A selection of bottle brushes.

Sometimes, as explained in the section on the hydrometer, the density of a concentrate is given in terms other than specific gravity, perhaps according to the Baumé, Balling or Brix scales, and for the purposes of quick reference the following short tables will be useful:-

Tables of Gravity Equivalents

The Meaning of Baume		The Meaning of Brix	
Baume	Gravity	Balling or Brix	Gravity
34	306	65	316
35	318	66	322
36	330	67	329
37	343	68	335
38	355	69	341
39	368	70	347
40	381	71	353
41	394	72	360
42	407	73	366
43	421	74	372
		75	379
		77	392
		80	412

Production of Grape Concentrate Wine

In practice, the inexperienced winemaker may be guided by the following procedure which describes in detail the various steps involved in making wine from grape concentrate:

1. Wash and sterilize every item of equipment with the 10% stock solution of sulphite recommended in the section on sulphite. Rinse off any excess sulphite solution with cold water.

2. Prepare the must by mixing the contents of a can of grape concentrate with 4 cans of water in an open container such as a plastic bucket or dustbin. Stir vigorously to ensure that a completely homogeneous must is obtained.

3. Check the gravity of the must with a hydrometer. In most instances, it will be found to lie in the range 65-70, but when a high gravity concentrate has been used a higher value around 75-80 will be recorded. In the latter case, add an extra can of water (making 5 cans of water altogether) to reduce the gravity of the must to about 65.

4. Measure the acidity of the must by the method described previously. A well balanced must of this type should have an acid content of 4.0-5.5 ppt and acid must be added if less than 4.0 ppt are present. Since ¼ oz. acid blend per gallon (1½ gms. per litre) will increase the acidity by roughly 1.5 ppt, the amount required is easy to calculate. The beginner may initially prefer to omit this step and simply assume that the acid balance of the must is acceptable, which is often the case with good quality concentrates.

5. Adjust the initial gravity of the must to 80-90 by adding sugar at the rate of 10 oz. per gallon (60 gms. per litre). At the same time, add the nutrients and any acid which is required and stir until everything has completely dissolved.

6. Add an actively fermenting yeast starter and cover closely to exclude dust, insects and air-borne microbes.

7. Ferment in this open container for a few days until all foaming dies down, then transfer the fermenting must into a glass carboy fitted with a fermentation lock filled with 10% sulphite solution. Allow to ferment to dryness, at which point no more gas will be passing through the lock and the specific gravity of the must will be 0.990-0.995. This stage will take several weeks to complete.

8. Rack the new wine off the sediment within about a week of fermentation finishing and add ½ fl. oz. per gallon (2 mls. per litre) of stock sulphite solution. The container in which the wine is stored must be completely full to avoid spoilage, so that it should be racked into gallon jars or a number of bottles.

9. Rack for a second time as soon as a heavy deposit is noticed or after 6-8 weeks, whichever is the sooner, and add ¼ fl. oz. per gallon (1 ml. per litre) stock sulphite solution. Rack thereafter every 2-3 months until the wine throws no more lees and is crystal clear.

10. Bottle the wine when it is clear and has been stored for 3-6 months in bulk. Wine produced from grape concentrate is often pleasant to drink while it is quite young, but it is preferable to wait until the wine is at least 4-6 months old before trying it.

CHAPTER 3

Frozen and Canned Fruit Concentrates

The immense popularity enjoyed by grape concentrate tends to hide the fact that there are numerous other fruit juice concentrates which are also excellent for winemaking purposes. Another reason why these concentrates have been largely overlooked is because, until recently, comparatively few of them were stocked by suppliers of winemaking accessories, the main exceptions being apple and fig concentrates which have long been readily available from these sources. Now that winemakers are beginning to demand more variety than grape concentrate alone can offer, the more progressive retailers are expanding their range of products to include concentrates prepared from such popular fruits as apricots, cherries, raspberries and the like.

Many winemakers have also discovered that the freezer chests which are nowadays prominent features in most supermarkets are prolific sources of fruit concentrates. Although at one time orange juice was about the only fruit juice obtainable as a frozen concentrate, the great advances which recent years have seen in the technology of fruit juice concentration have resulted in a large selection of fruit juices being offered in this form. Thus, it is now possible to buy apple, orange, grapefuit, and pineapple juices and an orange/grapefruit blend as frozen concentrates, and the prospects are very good that others will appear on the market in the relatively near future.

Frozen concentrates have several advantages over the concentrates and canned juices. Since they are stored in the frozen stage at a temperature too low to permit bacterial or fungal development, little or no preservative which could inhibit or interfere with yeast growth is required. The winemaker consequently need have no fears of fermentation sticking on this account, as sometimes happens with canned juices. Price is another attractive feature, for supermarkets operate on the principle of low mark-ups and high sales volume which means that frozen concentrates purchased there are particularly good value for money.

Perhaps the most attractive feature of frozen concentrates is the high quality of the juice reconstituted from them, for it closely resembles juice freshly expressed from the fruit itself. Indeed, it may well be better in many instances because the juice used to manufacture the concentrate comes from tree-ripened fruit picked at its peak and processed immediately. Fresh fruit of this quality simply cannot be obtained in areas remote from the orchards where it is grown, but its juice has now been brought within the reach of winemakers everywhere with the advent of frozen concentrates. It may seem strange that juice reconstituted from frozen concentrate is frequently better than that expressed from fresh fruit bought locally (but shipped in from elsewhere), yet a check on the sugar/acid balance of orange juice from these two sources soon reveals how much better and cheaper the juice from frozen concentrate actually can be. Moreover, it is far less laborious to prepare!

The high quality of frozen concentrate can be ascribed mainly to the mild conditions under which concentration is effected in modern vacuum distillation or freeze-drying plants. These techniques have now been so refined and sophisticated that they preserve the fresh fruit character of the juice much better than has previously been possible. The winemaker should nevertheless always bear in mind that they are not perfect in this respect, as years of experience and experiment with grape concentrate have amply demonstrated. In other words, juice expressed from freshly picked, tree-ripened fruit will be superior to that prepared from frozen concentrate.

Vacuum distillation has already been described in the chapter on grape concentrate, but a few words may be said here on the subject of freeze-drying. The concept of freeze-drying is very simple and the process itself has been used in laboratories for many years, but for various reasons it did not become feasible on a large scale commercial basis until well into the 1960s. Nowadays, of course, many common items are being freeze-dried, of which the most familiar examples are perhaps certain nationally advertised brands of instant coffee.

The first stage in freeze-drying is to freeze the freshly expressed juice into solid blocks which are next broken up into chunks and placed in a vacuum chamber. Once the lumps of frozen juice are under vacuum, they are exposed to a source of radiant heat which does not melt the ice but instead cause it to sublime, i.e. the ice passes directly into water vapour without first melting to form liquid water. The water vapour released in this fashion is then removed from the atmosphere within the chamber by means of a condenser, more sublimes to take its place and so on the process goes until the desired degree of concentration has been achieved. At this point, the vacuum is released, the product is removed from the vacuum chamber and finally packaged ready for shipping.

Concentrated fruit juices may be conveniently divided into two main categories. First of all, there are the frozen concentrates which are mass produced for sale in supermarkets and the like and are reconstituted by their customers primarily for consumption as fruit juice. Such concentrates have the advantage of being cheap and readily available almost everywhere, even in grocery stores equipped with a freezer chest, so that they obviously hold considerable appeal to the winemaker.

By their very nature, frozen concentrate must be restricted to those fruits which are grown commercially on a very large scale and whose juice is popular as a breakfast or other meal-time beverage. Their comparatively low cost depends entirely upon the fact that the fruit is cheap to grow and that the frozen concentrate prepared from its juice enjoys immense sales. Orange juice is a typical case in point, for so much is sold that there are literally dozens of proprietary brands of frozen orange concentrate being successfully promoted throughout Britain.

Unfortunately, many fruits which make excellent wine are unlikely ever to appear as frozen concentrates, mainly because the fruit is either too expensive to grow or it is not planted extensively enough to make it economically feasible to offer its juice in this form. Since winemakers have a rather different set of values, however, the higher cost of a particular fruit concentrate may well be outweighed by the quality of the wine which can be produced from it. Under these circumstances, it is worth paying a premium price for the more exotic canned fruit concentrates prepared from such popular winemaking fruits as cherries, elderberries, blackberries, raspberries, blackcurrants and so on.

The first step when making wine from any type of concentrate is to determine how much sugar and acid it will contribute to the must.

Perhaps the most interesting point to note here is that the composition of a popular frozen concentrate such as orange or grapefruit concentrate does not normally vary very much from one brand to another. The vast majority, whether sweetened or unsweetened, fall within the gravity range 170-200, and an acidity range of 28-56 ppt. expressed as tartaric acid (most are 39 or 40). The sugar and acid balance of the must thus remains much the same whatever brand is selected.

A final word should be said about the bouquet of wines produced from fruit concentrates. Because some of the volatile constituents of the juice which contribute towards the bouquet of the wine are lost during the concentration process, wines made exclusively from concentrates are apt to have little "nose". The winemaker should therefore be aware of this deficiency and rectify it by including in the must an ingredient such as elderflowers or rose petals which will greatly improve the bouquet of the wine.

CHAPTER 4

A Range of Recipes

There are nowadays so many concentrates, purées, dried fruits and flowers and so on available from stores specializing in winemaking supplies that a large variety of different wines can be produced from these ingredients alone. Moreover, it is much simpler and more convenient to use prepackaged ingredients of this type than to start from fresh fruit. For one thing, less equipment is required. Even more important is the fact that winemaking is brought within the reach of apartment dwellers with little space at their disposal, for a few gallons of wine can be made from concentrate in a corner of the kitchen or some other equally as obscure spot.

Although it is hard to visualize anything easier than making wine from concentrate, experience has shown that certain concentrates either alone or in combination with other ingredients are better than others for the production of specific types of wine. The following range of recipes illustrates these remarks very well and shows how to make a variety of pleasantly enjoyable wines from concentrates and other ingredients which most reputable suppliers of winemaking accessories stock regularly. Any not obtainable there, notably bananas and frozen fruit concentrates, can be purchased at a local supermarket.

It will also be noticed that yeast nutrients and acid are not included in all these recipes. The reason for omitting them is very simple. The suppliers of the concentrates featured in these recipes have already adjusted their nutrient and acid balance so that there is no need to add more of these ingredients at the time the must is being prepared.

PALE SHERRY-STYLE WINE

Imperial	Metric	
1 pt	570 mls	*Pale Sherry-Type Grape Concentrate*
1 oz.	30 gms.	*Gypsum*
¼ tsp.	¼ tsp.	*Pectic Enzyme*
¼ tsp.	¼ tsp.	*Yeast Energizer*
14 ozs.	400 gms.	*Sugar*
6½ pts.	3.75 l.	*Water*
		Sherry Yeast Starter

Dissolve the pectic enzyme, sugar and energizer in the water then blend in the grape concentrate. Sprinkle the gypsum over the surface of the must with constant stirring to distribute it evenly throughout the must. Most of this gypsum will not dissolve but simply sink to the bottom of the fermentation vessel, but an excess is needed in order to ensure that it interacts properly with certain components of the concentrate. Inoculate the must with the actively fermenting yeast starter. Allow to ferment to dryness and rack for the first time about a week after all yeast activity has ceased. Add ¼ fl. oz. (7 mls.) stock sulphite solution. Transfer into smaller containers which are only about two-thirds full and leave the new wine in them to age and oxidize for several months. No racking should be carried out during this period unless a heavy deposit builds up. Once the wine is judged to be mature enough, rack it from the storage vessels and add just enough sugar to dull its dry edge slightly, say 1-2 ozs. (30-55 gms.) Add either ¼ tsp. stabilizer or 1 crushed stabilizer tablet and bottle the wine. Serve lightly chilled as an aperitif.

PALE SHERRY-STYLE WINE

Imperial	Metric	
1 pt.	570 mls.	*Pale Sherry-Type Grape Concentrate*
1 oz.	30 gms.	*Gypsum*
¼ tsp.	¼ tsp.	*Pectic Enzyme*
1 tsp.	1 tsp.	*Yeast Nutrients*
½ tsp.	½ tsp.	*Yeast Energizer*
1¼ lbs.	570 gms.	*Sugar*
6½ pts.	3.75 l.	*Water*
		Sherry Yeast Starter

Add the pectic enzyme, nutrients, energizer and sugar to the water and stir vigorously until all these ingredients have completely dissolved. Blend in the grape concentrate, then carefully sift in the gypsum. Stir the must continuously while adding the gypsum so that it is well mixed throughout the must. Although most of the gypsum will sink to the bottom of the container soon after it has been added, some will react with the cream of tartar already in the must. Once the gypsum has been incorporated, inoculate the must with the actively fermenting yeast starter. Leave it to ferment undisturbed until no more sugar remains and a dry wine is obtained. Rack the new wine for the first time about a week later and add ¼ fl. oz. (7 mls.) stock sulphite solution or 1 crushed Campden tablet. Store the wine in partly filled containers for the next few months without racking it so that it can develop a proper sherry character. Finally, rack it off its sediment when it has acquired sufficient sherry flavour and bouquet. Bottle the young wine at this point and mature in bottle for a little longer before serving delicately chilled as a dry aperitif.

FRENCH VERMOUTH-STYLE WINE

Imperial	Metric	
1 pt.	*570 mls.*	*French Vermouth-Type Grape Concentrate*
½ tsp.	*½ tsp.*	*Tannin*
¼ tsp.	*¼ tsp.*	*Pectic Enzyme*
1 tsp.	*1 tsp.*	*Yeast Nutrients*
½ tsp.	*½ tsp.*	*Yeast Energizer*
1½ lbs.	*675 gms.*	*Sugar*
6 pts	*3.5 l.*	*Water*
		General Purpose Yeast Starter

Add the sugar, pectic enzyme, tannin, nutrients and energizer to the water and stir until everything has completely dissolved. Blend in the grape concentrate and mix thoroughly. Inoculate the must with the actively fermenting yeast starter. Set it aside to ferment undisturbed until no more sugar remains and a dry wine is obtained. Wait for about a week before racking it for the first time so that much of the suspended matter has a chance to settle out. Add ½ fl. oz. (15 mls.) stock sulphite solution or 2 crushed Campden tablets. Carry out a second racking as soon as a thick sediment is noticed or after 2 months if only a small deposit builds up. This wine will generally be clear and ready for bottling by the time its third racking falls due in another 3 months. Add just enough sugar to blunt its dry edge followed by ¼ fl. oz. (7 mls.) stock sulphite solution and 1 crushed stabilizer tablet to inhibit further fermentation. Bottle the young wine at this stage and leave it for another month or two to mature in bottle before serving as an aperitif.

WHITE PORT-STYLE WINE

Imperial	Metric	
1 pt	570 mls	White Port-Type Grape Concentrate
1 tsp.	1 tsp.	Tannin
¼ tsp.	¼ tsp.	Pectic Enzyme
½ tsp.	½ tsp.	Yeast Energizer
6 pts.	3.5 l.	Water
		Sugar as required
		Port Yeast Starter

Add the tannin, pectic enzyme, energizer and 1½ lbs. sugar to the water and stir vigorously until all these ingredients have dissolved. Mix in the grape concentrate, then inoculate the must with the actively fermenting yeast starter. Once fermentation begins, start checking the gravity periodically until a reading of 5 is recorded. At this point, add 4 ozs. (110 gms.) sugar, preferably as a strong syrup, and leave the fermentation to proceed. Continue checking the gravity in this way and feed the yeast with 4 ozs. (110 gms.) sugar every time it drops to 5 until fermentation finally comes to an end. Wait for about a week while much of the suspended matter settles, then rack for the first time. Treat the new wine with ½ fl. oz. (15 mls.) stock sulphite solution or 2 crushed Campden tablets. Rack it again in another 2 months or sooner if a heavy sediment accumulates. At the third racking in a further 3 months, add ¼ lb. (110 gms.) sugar followed by ¼ fl. oz. (7 mls.) stock sulphite solution and 1 crushed stabilizer tablet. Bottle the wine at this stage and age it in bottle for a little longer before serving well chilled as an aperitif.

RED VERMOUTH-STYLE WINE

Imperial	Metric	
1 pt	*570 mls*	*Red Vermouth-Type Grape Concentrate*
1 tsp.	*1 tsp.*	*Tannin*
¼ tsp.	*¼ tsp.*	*Pectic Enzyme*
½ tsp.	*½ tsp*	*Yeast Energizer*
6 pts.	*3.5 l.*	*Water*
		Sugar as required
		General Purpose Yeast Starter

Mix the concentrate with the water in which all the other ingredients except the yeast starter have already been dissolved. Add 1 lb. (450 gms.) sugar and stir vigorously until it has completely dissolved. Inoculate the must with the actively fermenting yeast starter. Once fermentation commences, check the gravity regularly until a reading of about 5 is recorded. At this point, add 4 ozs. (110 gms.) sugar, preferably in the form of a heavy syrup, and mix it in thoroughly. Allow fermentation to continue and repeat this procedure every time the gravity drops to 5 until the yeast reaches its maximum alcohol tolerance and the must stops fermenting. Rack the new wine for the first time about a week later and add ½ fl. oz. stock sulphite solution (15 mls.) or 2 crushed Campden tablets. The second racking should be carried out as soon as a heavy deposit is observed or after 2 months if little sediment accumulates. Rack it for the third time in another 3 months and add 1 lb. (450 gms.) sugar. Stir the wine until all this sugar has dissolved. Add ¼ fl. oz. (7 mls.) stock sulphite solution or 1 crushed Campden tablet and ¼ tsp. stabilizer or 1 crushed stabilizer tablet to ensure that no fermentation recurs. Bottle the young wine and allow it to age for a little longer in bottle.

ITALIAN VERMOUTH-STYLE WINE

Imperial	Metric	
1 pt.	*570 mls.*	*Italian Vermouth-Type Grape Concentrate*
½ tsp.	*½ tsp.*	*Tannin*
¼ tsp.	*¼ tsp.*	*Pectic Enzyme*
1 tsp.	*1 tsp.*	*Yeast Nutrients*
½ tsp.	*½ tsp.*	*Yeast Energizer*
6 pts.	*3.5 l.*	*Water*
		Sugar as required
		General Purpose Yeast Starter

Add the tannin, pectic enzyme, nutrients, energizer and 1 lb. (450 gms.) sugar to the water and stir vigorously until everything has completely dissolved. Blend in the grape concentrate, then introduce the actively fermenting yeast starter. Allow fermentation to proceed until the hydrometer shows a gravity reading of about 5. Once this stage is reached, add 4 ozs. (110 gms.) sugar, preferably in the form of a heavy syrup, and let fermentation continue. Check the gravity periodically until a reading of about 5 is again recorded, then add another 4 ozs. (110 gms) sugar as before. Repeat this procedure every time the gravity drops to 5 until the yeast reaches its maximum alcohol tolerance and fermentation finally ceases. Rack the new wine about a week later and add ½ fl. oz. (15 mls.) stock sulphite solution or 2 crushed Campden tablets. Rack it again as soon as a heavy sediment is observed or after 2 months if only a small lees forms. Sweeten the wine to taste with sugar syrup following the third racking in another 3 months and treat it with ¼ fl. oz. (7 mls) stock sulphite solution or 1 crushed Campden tablet. A crushed stabilizer tablet should also be added to prevent fermentation from restarting. Bottle the sweetened wine and allow it to age for another month or two in bottle before serving.

WHITE TABLE WINE

Imperial	Metric	
1 pt	*570 mls*	*White Grape Concentrate*
½ tsp.	*½ tsp.*	*Acid Blend*
¼ tsp.	*¼ tsp.*	*Tannin*
¼ tsp.	*¼ tsp.*	*Pectic Enzyme*
1 tsp.	*1 tsp.*	*Yeast Nutrients*
¼ tsp.	*¼ tsp.*	*Yeast Energizer*
10 ozs.	*275 gms.*	*Sugar*
6½ pts.	*3,75 l.*	*Water*
		General Purpose Yeast Starter

Dilute the concentrate with the water, then add all the other ingredients except the yeast starter. Stir vigorously until everything has completely dissolved. Introduce the actively fermenting yeast starter. Leave the must to ferment to dryness and allow it to stand undisturbed for about a week after all yeast activity has ceased so that clarification can commence. Rack the new wine and add ½ fl. oz. (15 mls.) stock sulphite solution or 2 crushed Campden tablets. A second racking will be required in another 2 months or sooner if a thick deposit forms. This wine will usually be bright and clear by the time it is due for its third racking in another 3 months. Should a faint haze still be present at that time, clarify the wine with a reliable proprietary fining agent before proceeding further. Bottle the clear wine and leave it for a few months in bottle to mature before serving well chilled as a white table wine.

WHITE TABLE WINE

Imperial	Metric	
30 fl. oz.	850 mls.	Spanish White Grape Concentrate
¾ oz.	20 gms	Acid Blend
1 tsp.	1 tsp.	Tannin
¼ tsp.	¼ tsp.	Pectic Enzyme
2 tsp.	2 tsp	Yeast Nutrients
¼ tsp.	¼ tsp.	Yeast Energizer
8 ozs.	225 gms	Sugar
10 pts.	5.75 l.	Water
		General Purpose Yeast Starter

Thin the consistency of the concentrate by standing the can in a pan of hot water for a short time before it is opened. Add the contents to the water in which all the other ingredients except the yeast starter have already been dissolved. Stir vigorously until the concentrate has completely dispersed. Inoculate the must with the actively fermenting yeast starter. Allow to ferment to dryness and rack the new wine for the first time about a week later. Add ½ fl. oz. (15 mls.) stock sulphite solution or 2 crushed Campden tablets. Rack again as soon as a heavy deposit has built up or after 2 months if only a little sediment settles out. This wine may still be slightly hazy by the time its third racking falls due in another 3 months. In that case, clarify it by means of a reliable proprietary fining agent. Treat the clear wine with ¼ fl. oz. (7 mls.) stock sulphite solution or 1 crushed Campden tablet. Bottle it at this stage and allow to mature in bottle for a few months longer before serving well chilled.

WHITE TABLE WINE

Imperial	Metric	
1 pt.	570 mls.	White Grape Concentrate
¼ tsp.	¼ tsp.	Tannin
¼ tsp.	¼ tsp.	Pectic Enzyme
1 tsp.	1 tsp.	Yeast Nutrients
¼ tsp.	¼ tsp.	Yeast Energizer
14 ozs.	400 gms.	400
6 ½ pts.	3.75 l.	Steinberg Yeast Starter
		Steinberg Yeast Starter

Add the tannin, pectic enzyme, nutrients, energizer and sugar to about half a gallon (2 litres) of water and stir until everything has completely dissolved. Blend in the concentrate together with the rest of the water. Introduce the actively fermenting yeast starter. Leave the must to ferment to dryness and rack the new wine for the first time about a week later when much of the suspended yeast has settled out. Add ½ fl. oz. (15 mls.) stock sulphite solution or 2 crushed Campden tablets. Rack again as soon as a heavy sediment is observed or after 2 months if only a small deposit forms. If this wine is not completely clear by the time the third racking falls due in another 3 months, fine it with a reliable proprietary fining agent. Add 2 oz. (55 gms.) sugar and stir until it has all dissolved. Protect the wine against refermentation by adding ¼ fl. oz. (7 mls.) stock sulphite solution together with 1 crushed stabilizer tablet. Bottle the young wine and mature for another month or two before serving well chilled as a white table wine.

MOSELLE-STYLE WINE

Imperial	Metric	
1 pt	570 mls	Moselle-Type Grape Concentrate
¼ tsp.	¼ tsp	Tannin
¼ tsp.	¼ tsp.	Pectic Enzyme
¼ tsp.	¼ tsp.	Yeast Energizer
7 ozs.	200 gms.	Sugar
6½ pts.	3.75 l.	Water
		Moselle Yeast Starter

Blend the grape concentrate with the water in which all the other ingredients except the yeast starter have already been dissolved. Inoculate the must with the actively fermenting yeast starter. Allow the fermentation to proceed undisturbed until no more sugar remains and a dry wine is achieved. Wait for about a week before racking the wine for the first time in order that as much as possible of the yeast and other debris in suspension will have a chance to settle out. Add ½ fl. oz. (15 mls.) stock sulphite solution or 2 crushed Campden tablets. Rack the wine again as soon as a heavy sediment is observed or after 2 months and add ¼ fl. oz. stock sulphite solution. This wine may still be faintly hazy by the time the third racking falls due in another 3 months. In that case, treat it with a reliable proprietary fining agent to clarify it. Sweeten the clear wine slightly with 2 ozs. (55 gms.) sugar and add ¼ fl. oz. (7 mls.) stock sulphite solution plus ¼ tsp. stabilizer to prevent any subsequent refermentation. Bottle the wine at this point and allow it to age for a month or two longer in bottle before serving it well chilled on a warm summer day.

MOSELLE-STYLE WINE

Imperial	Metric	
40 fl. oz.	1130 mls	Moselle-Type Grape Concentrate
¼ tsp.	¼ tsp.	Tannin
¼ tsp.	¼ tsp.	Pectic Enzyme
¼ tsp.	¼ tsp.	Yeast Energizer
3 qts	3.5 l.	Water
		Zeltinger Yeast Starter

Mix the tannin, pectic enzyme and energizer with the water and stir vigorously until all these ingredients have gone into solution. Add the grape concentrate and continue stirring until it too has dissolved. Introduce the actively fermenting yeast starter and allow fermentation to proceed undisturbed. Once fermentation comes to an end, set the new wine aside for about a week so that the yeast and other material in suspension can settle out. Rack it at this point and add ½ fl. oz. (15 mls.) stock sulphite solution or 2 crushed Campden tablets. Rack for the second time as soon as a heavy sediment is observed or after 2 months if only a small deposit forms. Should this wine still be slightly hazy by the time it is due for its third racking in a further 3 months, clarify it by means of a reliable proprietary fining agent. Sweeten the wine slightly with 2-4 ozs. (55-110 gms.) sugar, then add ¼ fl. oz. (7 mls.) stock sulphite solution plus ¼ tsp. stabilizer to ensure that no inconvenient refermentation will subsequently take place. Bottle the young wine and allow it to mature for a month or two longer in bottle. Serve well chilled.

HOCK-STYLE WINE

Imperial	Metric	
1 pt	570 mls	Hock-Type Grape Concentrate
¼ tsp.	¼ tsp.	Tannin
¼ tsp.	¼ tsp.	Pectic Enzyme
¼ tsp.	¼ tsp.	Yeast Energizer
½ lb.	225 gms.	Sugar
6½ pts	3.75 l.	Water
		Rhine Yeast Starter

Add the sugar, tannin, pectic enzyme and energizer to the water and stir vigorously until all these ingredients have dissolved. Mix in the grape concentrate followed by the actively fermenting yeast starter. Once fermentation starts, allow it to go to dryness when all yeast activity will cease. At this point, leave the new wine to stand undisturbed for about a week so that much of the suspended yeast can settle out. Rack the new wine and add ½ fl. oz. (15 mls.) stock sulphite solution or 2 crushed Campden tablets. A second racking will be required as soon as a heavy deposit is noticed or after 2 months if only a little sediment accumulates. This wine will usually be bright and clear by the time its third racking falls due. Sweeten it sightly following this racking by adding 2-4 ozs. (55-110 gms.) sugar, preferably in the form of a heavy syrup, to dull the dry edge of the wine. Make sure that it does not ferment at a later date by adding ¼ fl. oz. (7 mls.) stock sulphite solution together with ¼ tsp. stabilizer. Bottle the young wine and allow it to age in bottle for a few months longer. Serve well chilled.

HOCK-STYLE WINE

Imperial	Metric	
4 pts	2.25 l.	*Hock-Type Grape Concentrate*
½ tsp.	½ tsp.	*Tannin*
¼ tsp.	¼ tsp.	*Pectic Enzyme*
2 tsp.	2 tsp.	*Yeast Nutrients*
½ tsp.	½ tsp.	*Yeast Energizer*
1½ gal.	6.75 l.	*Water*
		Rhine Yeast Starter

Dissolve the tannin, pectic enzyme, nutrients and energizer in the water, then blend in the grape concentrate. Inoculate the must with the actively fermenting yeast starter. Allow fermentation to proceed undisturbed until the yeast has utilized all the sugar and a dry wine is obtained. Let the wine settle for about a week before racking it for the first time. Add 1 fl. oz. (30 mls.) stock sulphite solution or the equivalent in crushed Campden tablets. Rack for the second time in another 2 months or sooner if a thick sediment is noticed. If this wine has not cleared to brilliance by the time its third racking falls due in another 3 months, clarify it by means of a reliable proprietary fining agent. Sweeten the clear wine slightly with about 4 ozs (110 gms.) sugar, then add ½ fl. oz. (15 mls.) stock sulphite solution together with 2 crushed stabilizer tablets to prevent refermentation. Bottle the wine at this point and leave it to mature in bottle for a little longer before serving well chilled.

HOCK-STYLE WINE

Imperial	Metric	
1 pt	570 mls	*Hock or Riesling-Type Grape Concentrate*
1 tsp.	1 tsp.	*Acid Blend*
¼ tsp.	¼ tsp.	*Tannin*
¼ tsp.	¼ tsp.	*Pectic Enzyme*
1 tsp.	1 tsp.	*Yeast Nutrients*
¼ tsp.	¼ tsp.	*Yeast Energizer*
8 ozs.	225 gms.	*Sugar*
6½ pts.	3.75 l.	*Water*
		Steinberg Yeast Starter

Add the acid blend, tannin, pectic enzyme, nutrients, energizer and sugar to about half a gallon of the water (2 litres) and stir until all these ingredients have completely dissolved. Carefully mix in the grape concentrate, then add the balance of the water and continue stirring until the must is homogeneous. Add the actively fermenting yeast starter. Allow the must to ferment to dryness and rack it for the first time about a week later when much of the yeast will have settled out. Add ½ fl. oz. (15 mls.) stock sulphite solution or 2 crushed Campden tablets. Rack for the second time in another 2 months or sooner if a thick deposit is observed. If this wine is still faintly hazy by the time its third racking falls due in another 3 months, clarify it with the aid of a reliable proprietary fining agent. Sweeten the clear wine slightly with 2-4 ozs. (55-110 gms.) sugar according to taste and add ¼ fl. oz. (7 mls.) stock sulphite solution or 1 crushed Campden tablet followed by ¼ tsp. stabilizer to prevent any inconvenient refermentation. Bottle the young wine at this point and set it aside for a few more months to acquire some bottle age. Serve well chilled as a delicate white table wine.

RHINE-STYLE WINE

Imperial	Metric	
1 pt.	570 mls.	Riesling-Type Grape Concentrate
¼ tsp.	¼ tsp.	Tannin
¼ tsp.	¼ tsp.	Pectic Enzyme
1 tsp.	1 tsp.	Yeast Nutrients
¼ tsp.	¼ tsp.	Yeast Energizer
14 ozs.	400 gms.	Sugar
6½ pts.	3.75 l.	Water
		Rhine Yeast Starter

Add all the ingredients except the grape concentrate and yeast starter to the water and stir vigorously until everything has completely dissolved. Blend in the grape concentrate then inoculate the must with the actively fermenting yeast starter. Leave the must to ferment to dryness. After all yeast activity has ceased, leave the new wine to stand undisturbed for about a week so that much of the matter in suspension can settle out. Rack the wine at this point and add ½ fl. oz. (15 mls.)

stock sulphite solution or 2 crushed Campden tablets. Rack it for the second time as soon as a thick deposit is noticed or after 2 months if only a little sediment accumulates. This wine will normally be bright and clear by the time it is due for its third racking in another 3 months. Should a faint haze still persist, clarify the wine with the aid of a reliable proprietary fining agent. Sweeten the clear wine slightly with 4 ozs. (110 gms.) sugar and add ¼ fl. oz. (7 mls.) stock sulphite solution or 1 crushed Campden tablet together with 1 crushed stabilizer tablet. Bottle the wine and leave it to age in bottle for a month or two longer before serving it well chilled as a white table wine.

RHINE-STYLE WINE

Imperial	Metric	
40 fl. ozs.	*1130 mls*	*Riesling-Type Grape Concentrate*
¼ tsp.	*¼ tsp.*	*Tannin*
¼ tsp.	*¼ tsp.*	*Pectic Enzyme*
¼ tsp.	*¼ tsp.*	*Yeast Energizer*
3 qts.	*3.5 l.*	*Water*
		Johannisberger Yeast Starter

Add the tannin, pectic enzyme and yeast energizer to the water and stir until these ingredients have all dissolved. Mix in the grape concentrate and continue stirring until it has been properly incorporated. Inoculate the must with the actively fermenting yeast starter. Set it aside to ferment undisturbed until no more sugar remains and fermentation comes to an end. Wait for about a week while much of the suspended yeast and other insoluble material settles out before racking for the first time. Add ¼ fl. oz. (15 mls.) stock sulphite solution or 2 crushed Campden tablets. Rack again as soon as a heavy sediment is noticed or after 2 months if only a small deposit forms. This wine will normally be quite clear by the time its third racking falls due in another 3 months. Should a faint haze still remain at this point, clarify the wine with the aid of a reliable proprietary fining agent. Sweeten the wine slightly with 4 ozs. (110 gms.) sugar in the form of a heavy syrup, then add ¼ fl. oz. (7 mls.) stock sulphite solution and 1 crushed stabilizer tablet to prevent refermentation. Bottle the clear wine at this stage and allow it to age for another few months in bottle before serving well chilled as a white table wine.

LIEBFRAUMILCH-STYLE WINE

Imperial	Metric	
1 pt	*570 mls*	*Liebfraumilch-Type Grape Concentrate*
¼ tsp.	*¼ tsp.*	*Tannin*
¼ tsp.	*¼ tsp.*	*Pectic Enzyme*
¼ tsp.	*¼ tsp.*	*Yeast Energizer*
9 ozs.	*250 gms.*	*Sugar*
6½ pts.	*3.75 l.*	*Water*
		Rhine Yeast Starter

Dissolve the tannin, pectic enzyme, energizer and sugar in the water, then blend in the grape concentrate. Introduce the actively fermenting yeast starter. Leave the must to ferment undisturbed until the yeast has utilized all the sugar and a dry wine remains. Wait for about a week to let the suspended yeast and other debris settle out before racking the new wine. Treat it with ½ fl. oz. (15 mls.) stock sulphite solution or 2 crushed Campden tablets. The second racking should be carried out as soon as a thick deposit is noticed or after 2 months if only a small lees forms. Add ¼ fl. oz. (7 mls.) stock sulphite solution. This wine will usually be clear when its third racking is due in another 3 months, but it should be clarified with a reliable proprietary finings if a faint haze still persists. Sweeten the wine with 4 ozs. (110 gms.) sugar at this point and protect it against renewed fermentation by adding ¼ fl. oz. stock sulphite solution and ¼ tsp. stabilizer. Bottle the wine at this stage and allow it to acquire a little bottle age before serving it well chilled.

GRAVES-STYLE WINE

Imperial	Metric	
1 pt	*570 mls*	*Graves-Type Grape Concentrate*
¼ tsp.	*¼ tsp.*	*Tannin*
¼ tsp.	*¼ tsp.*	*Pectic Enzyme*
¼ tsp.	*¼ tsp.*	*Yeast Energizer*
11 ozs.	*310 gms.*	*Sugar*
6½ pts.	*3.75 l.*	*Water*
		Bordeaux Yeast Starter

Add all the ingredients except the grape concentrate and yeast starter to about half a gallon of water and stir vigorously until they have completely dissolved. Mix in the grape concentrate together with the rest of the water and stir the must thoroughly. Inoculate it with the actively fermenting yeast starter. Allow fermentation to proceed undisturbed until the yeast has utilized all the sugar and a dry wine is obtained. Rack the new wine for the first time about a week later when much of the suspended yeast will have settled out. Add ½ fl. oz. (15 mls.) stock sulphite solution or 2 crushed Campden tablets. Rack again in another 2 months or sooner if a heavy sediment is noticed. This wine will probably be perfectly clear by the time it is due for its third racking in another 3 months, but sometimes a faint haze will remain. In that case, clarify the wine with the aid of a reliable proprietary fining agent. Add 2 ozs (55 gms.) sugar to dull its dry edge followed by ¼ fl. oz. (7 mls.) stock sulphite solution. Either ¼ tsp. stabilizer or 1 crushed stabilizer tablet should also be added to prevent any subsequent refermentation. Bottle the clear wine and allow to age for another few months in bottle before serving well chilled.

GRAVES-STYLE WINE

Imperial	Metric	
4 pts.	2.25 l.	*Graves-Type Grape Concentrate*
½ tsp.	½ tsp.	*Tannin*
¼ tsp.	¼ tsp.	*Pectic Enzyme*
2 tsp.	2 tsp.	*Yeast Nutrients*
½ tsp.	½ tsp.	*Yeast Energizer*
1½ gal.	6.75 l.	*Water*
		Graves Yeast Starter

Add the tannin, pectic enzyme, nutrients and energizer to the water and stir vigorously until all these ingredients have completely dissolved. Blend in the grape concentrate, then inoculate the must with the actively fermenting yeast starter. Leave to ferment undisturbed until the yeast has utilized all the sugar and a dry wine remains. Rack the new wine for the first time about a week later when much of the suspended matter will have settled out. Add 1 fl. oz. (30 mls.) stock sulphite solution or the equivalent in crushed Campden tablets. Rack again in another 2 months or sooner if a heavy sediment builds up. If this wine has not cleared to briliance by the time its third racking falls due in another 3 months, clarify it by means of a reliable proprietary finings. Sweeten the young wine slightly with about 4 ozs. (110 gms.) sugar, then add ½ fl. oz. (15 mls.) stock sulphite solution together with 2 crushed stabilizer tablets to protect it from renewed fermentation. Bottle the wine at this point and allow it to age in bottle for a month or two longer before serving well chilled.

GRAVES-STYLE WINE

Imperial	Metric	
2.2 lb.	1 kg.	Graves-Type Grape Concentrate
½ tsp.	½ tsp.	Acid Blend
¼ tsp.	¼ tsp.	Tannin
¼ tsp.	¼ tsp.	Pectic Enzyme
1 tsp.	1 tsp.	Yeast Nutrients
¼ tsp.	¼ tsp.	Yeast Energizer
11 ozs.	310 gms.	Sugar
6½	3.75 l.	Water
		Bordeaux Yeast Starter

Blend the grape concentrate with the water in which all the other ingredients except the yeast starter have already been dissolved. Add the actively fermenting yeast starter. Leave the must to ferment undisturbed until the yeast has utilized all the sugar and a dry wine remains. Rack the new wine for the first time about a week later after much of the yeast and other matter in suspension has had time to settle out. Treat the wine with ½ fl. oz. (15 mls.) stock sulphite solution or 2 crushed Campden tablets. Rack it for the second time as soon as a thick deposit is observed or after another 2 months if only a thin sediment builds up. This wine may still be slightly hazy by the time the third racking falls due in another 3 months, in which case it should be clarified by means of a reliable proprietary fining agent. Sweeten the clear wine slightly with 4 ozs. (110 gms.) sugar and add ¼ fl. oz. (7 mls.) stock sulphite solution plus 1 crushed stabilizer tablet to protect it against the risk of renewed fermentation. Bottle the wine at this point and allow it to mature in bottle for a few more months before serving it as a white table wine.

CHABLIS-STYLE WINE

Imperial	Metric	
1 pt	*570 mls*	*Chablis-Type Grape Concentrate*
¼ tsp.	*¼ tsp.*	*Tannin*
¼ tsp.	*¼ tsp.*	*Pectic Enzyme*
¼ tsp.	*¼ tsp.*	*Yeast Energizer*
12 ozs.	*350 gms.*	*Sugar*
6½ pts.	*3.75 l.*	*Water*
		Burgundy Yeast Starter

Dilute the concentrate with the water in which all the other ingredients except the yeast starter have already been dissolved. Mix thoroughly, then inoculate the must with the actively fermenting yeast starter. Leave the must to ferment undisturbed until the yeast has utilized all the sugar and a dry wine is obtained. Rack the new wine for the first time about a week later when much of the suspended yeast will have settled out. Add ½ fl. oz. (15 mls.) stock sulphite solution. Rack again in another 2 months or as soon as a heavy sediment is observed. A third racking will be needed in another 3 months by which time the wine should be bright and clear. If a faint haze still persists at this stage, clarify the wine with the aid of a reliable proprietary fining agent. Add ¼ fl. oz. (7 mls.) stock sulphite solution or 1 crushed stabilizer tablet to protect it against the risk of renewed fermentation. Bottle the wine at this point and allow it to mature in bottle for a few more months before serving it as a white table wine.

CHAMPAGNE-STYLE WINE

Imperial	Metric	
1 pt.	*570 mls.*	*Champagne-Type Grape Concentrate*
¼ tsp.	*¼ tsp.*	*Pectic Enzyme*
1 tsp.	*1 tsp.*	*Yeast Nutrients*
¼ tsp.	*¼ tsp.*	*Yeast Energizer*
15 ozs.	*425 gms.*	*Sugar*
6½ pts.	*3.75 l.*	*Water*
		Champagne Yeast Starter

Mix the grape concentrate with the water in which all the other ingredients except the yeast starter have already been dissolved. Add the actively fermenting yeast starter. Leave the must to ferment until the yeast has utilized all the sugar and a dry wine is obtained. Set it aside to stand undisturbed for about a week before racking it for the first time so that much of the yeast and other suspended matter has a chance to settle out. Add ¼ fl. oz. (7 mls.) stock sulphite solution or 2 crushed Campden tablets. Rack it again as soon as a heavy sediment is noticed or after 2 months if only a small deposit forms. Clarify the wine at this point with the aid of a reliable proprietary fining agent. Dissolve exactly 3 ozs. (85 gms.) sugar in the clear wine and bottle it at once. Wire the corks down and transfer the bottles into cool surroundings. There will normally still be enough yeast cells in the wine to ensure that the desired fermentation takes place in the bottles during the next 4-6 months. If the bottles are allowed to stand upright throughout this period, the thin layer of yeast will settle out in the bottom of the bottles. The contents can then be poured out without disturbing this sediment if they are first well chilled and the bottle is emptied in one operation without being returned to the vertical position. This technique avoids the need to disgorge the sediment before serving the wine.

ROSÉ TABLE WINE

Imperial	Metric	
1 pt	570 mls	Rosé Grape Concentrate
½ tsp.	½ tsp.	Acid Blend
¼ tp.	¼ tsp.	Tannin
¼ tsp.	¼ tsp.	Pectic Enzyme
1 tsp.	1 tsp.	Yeast Nutrients
¼ tsp.	¼ tsp.	Yeast Energizer
9 ozs.	250 gms.	Sugar
6½ pts.	3.75 l.	Water
		General Purpose Yeast Starter

Add the grape concentrate to the water in which all the other ingredients except the yeast starter have already been dissolved. Stir vigorously, then inoculate the must with the actively fermenting yeast starter. Allow the must to ferment to dryness when the yeast will have utilized all the sugar and no more carbon dioxide is being evolved. At this point, leave the wine to stand undisturbed for about a week while much of the suspended yeast settles out, then rack it for the first time. Add ¼ fl. oz. (7 mls.) stock sulphite solution or 1 crushed Campden tablet. Rack again as soon as a heavy deposit is observed or after 2 months if only a little sediment accumulates. This wine may still be slightly hazy when its third racking falls due in another 3 months. If this is the case, clarify it with the aid of a reliable proprietary fining agent. Sweeten the clear wine slightly with 2-4 ozs. (55-110 gms.) sugar according to taste, then add ¼ fl. oz. (7 mls.) stock sulphite solution or 1 crushed Campden tablet together with ¼ tsp. stabilizer or 1 crushed stabilizer tablet. Bottle the young wine at this point and set it aside to age in bottle for a few months before serving lightly chilled.

ROSEBERRY ROSÉ

Imperial	Metric	
1 pt	570 mls	White Grape Concentrate
15 ozs.	425 gms.	Irish Rosehip Purée
1 lb.	450 gms.	Bananas
½ tsp.	½ tsp.	Tannin
¼ tsp.	¼ tsp.	Pectic Enzyme
2 tsp.	2 tsp.	Yeast Nutrients
½ tsp.	½ tsp.	Yeast Energizer
2¼ lbs.	1 kg.	Sugar
1¾ gal.	8 l.	Water
		Bordeaux Yeast Starter

Peel the bananas and cut the fruit into slices, discarding the skins. Boil the sliced fruit in about 1 quart (1 litre) of water for 20 minutes, then carefully strain off the spent pulp and discard it. Dissolve the pectic enzyme, tannin, nutrients, energizer and sugar in the balance of the water. Mix in the banana extract, grape concentrate and Rosehip purée and stir until the must is homogeneous. Introduce the actively fermenting yeast starter. Allow the must to ferment to dryness and rack the new wine for the first time about a week later when much of the suspended pulp particles will have settled to the bottom. Treat it with 1 fl. oz. (30 mls.) stock sulphite solution or 4 crushed Campden tablets.

Rack again as soon as a heavy sediment builds up and for the third time in another 3 months. If the wine is still faintly hazy at this point, clarify it with a reliable proprietary fining agent. Add ½ fl. oz. (15 mls) stock sulphite solution and ½ tsp. stabilizer after sweetening the wine with 8 ozs. (225 gms.) sugar. Bottle the young wine and leave it to mature in bottle for several more months. Serve well chilled as a rosé table wine.

ROSÉ TABLE WINE

Imperial	Metric	
1 pt.	570 mls.	Rosé Grape Concentrate
¼ tsp.	¼ tsp.	Tannin
¼ tsp.	¼ tsp.	Pectic Enzyme
1 tsp.	1 tsp.	Yeast Nutrients
¼ tsp.	¼ tsp.	Yeast Energizer
1 lb.	450 gms.	Sugar
6½ pts.	3.75 l.	Water
		General Purpose Yeast Starter

Add the tannin, pectic enzyme, nutrients, sugar and energizer to the water and stir vigorously until all these ingredients have gone into solution. Blend in the grape concentrate, then inoculate the must with the actively fermenting yeast starter. Leave the fermentation to proceed undisturbed until the yeast has utilized all the sugar and a dry wine is obtained. Let the new wine stand for about a week after all yeast activity has come to an end before racking it for the first time. Add ½ fl. oz. (15 mls.) stock sulphite solution or 2 crushed Campden tablets. Rack it again as soon as a thick deposit is observed. This wine will normally be quite clear by the time it is due for its third racking. Add 2-4 ozs. (55-110 gms.) sugar according to taste. Protect the wine against renewed fermentation by adding ¼ fl. oz. stock sulphite solution together with ¼ tsp. stabilizer or 1 crushed stabilizer tablet. Bottle the wine at this point and leave it to age in bottle for another month or two before serving lightly chilled.

ROSÉ TABLE WINE

Imperial	Metric	
40 fl. ozs.	1.13 l.	Rosé Grape Concentrate
¼ tsp.	¼ tsp.	Tannin
¼ tsp.	¼ tsp.	Pectic Enzyme
¼ tsp.	¼ tsp.	Yeast Energizer
3 qts.	3.5 l.	Water
		General Purpose Yeast Starter

Add all the ingredients except the yeast to the water and stir vigorously until everything has completely dissolved. Inoculate the must with the actively fermenting yeast starter. Leave to ferment undisturbed until no more sugar remains and yeast activity comes to a halt. Rack for the first time about a week later when much of the yeast and other suspended material has settled out. Treat the new wine with ½ fl. oz. (15 mls.) stock sulphite solution or 2 crushed Campden tablets. Rack again in a further 2 months or sooner if a heavy sediment accumulates. This wine will usually be quite clear by the time its third racking is due in another 3 months. If a faint haze still persists at this point, clarify the wine by means of a reliable proprietary fining agent. Sweeten the wine to taste with sugar syrup, then add ¼ fl. oz. (7 mls.) stock sulphite solution together with 1 crushed stabilizer tablet. Bottle the clear wine at this stage and leave it to mature in bottle for several months longer. Chill well before serving.

RED TABLE WINE

Imperial	Metric	
1 pt	570 mls	Red Grape Concentrate
¼ tsp.	¼ tsp.	Acid Blend
½ tsp.	½ tsp.	Tannin
¼ tsp.	¼ tsp.	Pectic Enzyme
1 tsp.	1 tsp.	Yeast Nutrients
¼ tsp.	¼ tsp.	Yeast Energizer
8 ozs.	225 gms.	Sugar
6½ pts.	3.75 l.	Water
		General Purpose Yeast Starter

Dissolve the acid blend, sugar, nutrients, energizer, pectic enzyme and tannin in the water, then mix in the red grape concentrate. Inoculate the must with the actively fermenting yeast starter. Leave it to ferment until no more sugar remains and all yeast activity comes to an end. Rack the new wine about a week later when much of the suspended yeast will have settled out. Add ½ fl. oz. (15 mls.) stock sulphite solution or 2 crushed Campden tablets. Rack again in another 2 months unless a thick deposit is observed sooner. This wine will normally be quite clear by the time it is ready for its third racking in another 3 months. Sulphite it lightly at this point with either ¼ fl. oz. (7 mls.) stock sulphite solution or 1 crushed Campden tablet. Bottle the young wine and allow it to mature in bottle for a few more months before serving it as a red table wine.

LIGHT RED TABLE WINE

Imperial	Metric	
30 fl. oz.	*850 mls.*	*Spanish Red Grape Concentrate*
½ oz.	*15 gms.*	*Acid Blend*
2 tsp.	*2 tsp.*	*Tannin*
¼ tsp.	*¼ tsp.*	*Pectic Enzyme*
2 tsp.	*2 tsp.*	*Yeast Nutrients*
½ tsp.	*½ tsp.*	*Yeast Energizer*
8 ozs.	*225 gms.*	*Sugar*
1¼ gal.	*5.75 l.*	*Water*
		Bordeaux Yeast Starter

Warm the concentrate by standing it in some hot water so that it pours more readily. In the meantime, add the acid blend, tannin, pectic enzyme, sugar, nutrients and energizer to the water and stir until all these ingredients have dissolved. Blend in the grape concentrate and stir vigorously. Inoculate the must with the actively fermenting yeast starter. Leave it to ferment until the yeast has utilized all the sugar and a dry wine remains. Wait for about a week after all yeast activity has ceased before racking the new wine so that much of the yeast held in suspension can settle to the bottom of the fermentation vessel. Rack the wine at this point and add ½ fl. oz. (15 mls.) stock sulphite solution or 2 crushed Campden tablets. A second racking will be required as soon as a heavy sediment is observed or after 2 months if only a small deposit forms. Rack for the third time in another 3 months and add ¼ fl. oz. (7 mls.) stock sulphite solution or 1 crushed Campden tablet. Bottle the wine at this stage and let it age in bottle for a little longer before serving as a red table wine.

RED TABLE WINE

Imperial	Metric	
30 fl. ozs.	850 mls.	Spanish Red Grape Concentrate
1½ tsp.	1½ tsp.	Acid Blend
½ tsp.	½ tsp.	Tannin
¼ tsp.	¼ tsp.	Pectic Enzyme
1 tsp.	1 tsp.	Yeast Nutrients
¼ tsp.	¼ tsp.	Yeast Energizer
6½ pts.	3.75 l.	Water
		General Purpose Yeast Starter

Stand the can of concentrate in some hot water for a time in order to thin the contents. During this time, dissolve the acid blend, tannin, pectic enzyme, nutrients and energizer in the water. Mix in the grape concentrate and stir vigorously until the must is homogeneous. Add the actively fermenting yeast starter. Allow the fermentation to proceed until no more sugar remains and a dry wine is obtained. Rack the new wine for the first time about a week later when much of the suspended matter has had a chance to settle out. Add ½ fl. oz. (15 mls.) stock sulphite solution or 2 crushed Campden tablets. Rack again in another 2 months or sooner if a thick deposit is noticed. This wine will normally be bright and clear by the time it is due for its third racking in a further 3 months. Add ¼ fl. oz. (7 mls.) stock sulphite solution or 1 crushed Campden tablet at this point. Bottle the clear wine and set it aside to age for a few more months before serving as a red table wine.

RED TABLE WINE

Imperial	Metric	
1 pt.	570 mls.	Red Grape Concentrate
½ tsp.	½ tsp.	Tannin
¼ tsp.	¼ tsp.	Pectic Enzyme
1 tsp.	1 tsp.	Yeast Nutrients
¼ tsp.	¼ tsp.	Yeast Energizer
1 lb.	450 gms.	Sugar
6½ pts.	3.75 l.	Water
		General Purpose Yeast Starter

Dissolve the tannin, pectic enzyme, nutrients, energizer and sugar in the water, then mix in the grape concentrate. Inoculate the must with the actively fermenting yeast starter. Allow fermentation to proceed until the yeast has utilized all the sugar and a dry wine is obtained. Rack the new wine about a week later when much of the suspended yeast and other matter has settled out. Add ½ fl. oz. (15 mls.) stock sulphite solution or 2 crushed Campden tablets. Rack for the second time as soon as a thick deposit is observed or after 2 months if little sediment accumulates. This wine will usually be bright and clear by the time its third racking falls due in another 3 months. Add ¼ fl. oz. (7 mls.) stock sulphite solution or 1 crushed Campden tablet. Bottle the wine at this point and leave it to age in bottle for several months before serving as a red table wine.

CLARET-STYLE WINE

Imperial	Metric	
1 pt	570 mls	Claret-Type Grape Concentrate
½ tsp.	½ tsp.	Tannin
¼ tsp.	¼ tsp.	Pectic Enzyme
¼ tsp.	¼ tsp.	Yeast Energizer
9 ozs.	250 gms.	Sugar
6½ pts.	3.75 l.	Water
		Bordeaux Yeast Starter

Blend the concentrate with the water then add the tannin, sugar, pectic enzyme, energizer and stir vigorously until all these ingredients have completely dissolved. Inoculate the must with the actively fermenting yeast starter. Leave it to ferment to dryness when all yeast activity will come to an end. Rack the new wine for the first time about a week later and add ½ fl. oz. (15 mls.) stock sulphite solution. A second racking will be needed in another 2 months or sooner if a thick sediment settles out. Rack for the third time in another 3 months and add ¼ fl. oz. stock sulphite solution (7 mls.) Bottle the young wine at this point and allow it to age in bottle for a few more months before serving it as a red table wine.

CLARET-STYLE WINE

Imperial	Metric	
4 pts.	2.25 l.	Red Bordeaux-Type Grape Concentrate
2 tsp.	2 tsp.	Tannin
¼ tsp.	¼ tsp.	Pectic Enzyme
2 tsp.	2 tsp.	Yeast Nutrients
½ tsp.	½ tsp.	Yeast Energizer
1¼ gal.	6.75 l.	Water
		Bordeaux Yeast Starter

Add the tannin, pectic enzyme, nutrients and energizer to the water and stir until everything has completely dissolved. Mix in the grape concentrate and stir vigorously until it has been incorporated properly into the must. Introduce the actively fermenting yeast starter. Allow the must to ferment undisturbed until no more sugar remains and a dry wine is obtained. Rack the new wine for the first time about a week later and add 1 fl. oz. (30 mls.) stock sulphite solution or the equivalent in crushed Campden tablets. Rack it again as soon as a thick deposit is noticed or after 2 months if only a little sediment accumulates. This wine will be quite clear by the time its third racking is due in another 3 months. Add ½ fl. oz. (15 mls.) stock sulphite solution or 2 crushed Campden tablets, then bottle the wine. Mature in bottle for a few more months before serving as a red table wine.

CLARET-STYLE WINE

Imperial	Metric	
1 pt	570 mls	Claret-Type Grape Concentrate
½ tsp.	½ tsp.	Acid Blend
½ tsp.	½ tsp.	Tannin
¼ tsp.	¼ tsp.	Pectic Enzyme
1 tsp.	1 tsp.	Yeast Nutrients
¼ tsp.	¼ tsp.	Yeast Energizer
10 ozs.	275 gms.	Sugar
6½ pts.	3.75 l.	Water
		Bordeaux Yeast Starter

Dilute the concentrate with the water and add all the other ingredients except the yeast starter. Stir vigorously until everything has dissolved. Add the actively fermenting yeast starter. Allow the must to ferment until the yeast has utilized all the sugar and it stops working. Wait for about a week after this stage is reached before racking the new wine for the first time. Sulphite it lightly at this point with ½ fl. oz. (15 mls.) stock sulphite solution or 2 crushed Campden tablets. Rack again in another 2 months or sooner if a heavy deposit forms. This wine will be ready for bottling by the time it is due for its third racking in another 3 months. Add ¼ fl. oz. (7 mls.) stock sulphite solution or 1 crushed Campden tablet, then bottle the wine. Allow to mature in bottle for a few more months before serving as a red table wine.

CLARET-STYLE WINE

Imperial	Metric	
40 fl. oz.	1.13 l.	Claret-Type Grape Concentrate
½ tsp.	½ tsp.	Tannin
¼ tsp.	¼ tsp.	Pectic Enzyme
¼ tsp.	¼ tsp.	Yeast Energizer
3 qts.	3.5 l.	Water
		Bordeaux Yeast Starter

Add all the ingredients except the yeast starter to the water and stir vigorously until everything has completely dissolved. Introduce the actively fermenting yeast starter. Allow fermentation to proceed until the yeast has utilized all the sugar and a dry wine is obtained. Leave the new wine to stand undisturbed for about a week so that much of the yeast and other insoluble material can settle out. Rack at this point and add ½ fl. oz. (15 mls.) stock sulphite solution or 2 crushed Campden tablets. Rack for the second time in 2 months or sooner if a thick deposit accumulates. This wine will usually be quite clear by the time it is due for its third racking in another 3 months. Add ¼ fl. oz. (7 mls.) stock sulphite solution or 1 crushed Campden tablet at this point, then bottle the wine. Mature in bottle for another couple of months at least before serving as a red table wine.

BEAUJOLAIS-STYLE WINE

Imperial	Metric	
1 pt	*570 mls*	*Beaujolais-Type Grape Concentrate*
½ tsp.	*½ tsp.*	*Tannin*
¼ tsp.	*¼ tsp.*	*Pectic Enzyme*
¼ tsp.	*¼ tsp.*	*Yeast Energizer*
10 ozs.	*275 gms.*	*Sugar*
6½ pts	*3.75 l.*	*Water*
		Beaujolais Yeast Starter

Add all the ingredients except the concentrate and yeast starter to the water and stir vigorously until all these ingredients have completely dissolved. Mix in the grape concentrate and again stir vigorously. Add the actively fermenting yeast starter. Allow fermentation to proceed until the yeast has utilized all the sugar and a dry wine is achieved. Leave it to stand undisturbed for about a week, then rack the new wine for the first time and add ½ fl. oz. (15 mls.) stock sulphite solution or 2 crushed Campden tablets. Rack it again as soon as a heavy sediment is observed or after another 2 months if only a small deposit forms. This wine will generally have clarified completely by the time its third racking falls due in another 3 months. Add ¼ fl. oz. stock sulphite solution (7 mls.) or 1 crushed Campden tablet, then bottle the wine. Age in bottle for a few more months before serving as a red table wine.

BEAUJOLAIS-STYLE WINE

Imperial	Metric	
4 pts.	2.25 l.	Beaujolais-Type Grape Concentrate
½ tsp.	½ tsp.	Tannin
¼ tsp.	¼ tsp.	Pectic Enzyme
2 tsp.	2 tsp.	Yeast Nutrients
½ tsp.	½ tsp.	Yeast Energizer
1½ gal.	6.75 l.	Water
		Beaujolais Yeast Starter

Add the grape concentrate to the water in which all the ingredients except the yeast starter have already been dissolved. Inoculate the must with the actively fermenting yeast starter. Leave it to ferment undisturbed until the yeast has utilized all the sugar and a dry wine is obtained. Rack the new wine for the first time about a week later when much of the yeast and other suspended matter will have settled out. Add 1 fl. oz. (30 mls.) stock sulphite solution or the equivalent in crushed Campden tablets. Rack for the second time in another 2 months or sooner if a heavy sediment accumulates. This wine will normally be clear and ready for bottling by the time its third racking falls due in a further 3 months. Add ½ fl. oz. (15 mls.) stock sulphite solution or 2 crushed Campden tablets and bottle the wine. Let it mature in bottle for a few more months before serving it as a red table wine.

BEAUJOLAIS-STYLE WINE

Imperial	Metric	
1 pt	570 mls	Beaujolais-Type Grape Concentrate
½ tsp.	½ tsp.	Acid Blend
¼ tsp.	¼ tsp.	Pectic Enzyme
1 tsp.	1 tsp.	Yeast Nutrients
¼ tsp.	¼ tsp.	Yeast Energizer
½ lb.	225 gms.	Sugar
6½ pts.	3.75 l.	Water
		Beaujolais Yeast Starter

Dissolve the sugar, acid blend, nutrients, energizer and pectic enzyme in about half a gallon (2 litres) of water, then add the Beaujolais type grape concentrate and mix thoroughly. Add the balance of the water and inoculate the must with the actively fermenting yeast starter. Allow the fermentation to proceed until no more sugar remains and yeast activity comes to an end. Rack the new wine for the first time about a week later and add ½ fl. oz. (15 mls.) stock sulphite solution or 2 crushed Campden tablets. Rack again as soon as a heavy deposit is observed or after 2 months if only a little sediment accumulates. This wine will usually be bright and clear by the time its third racking falls due in another 3 months. Add ¼ fl. oz. (7 mls.) stock sulphite solution or 1 crushed Campden tablet at this point. Bottle the wine at this stage and allow it to age in bottle for another few months before serving it as a red table wine.

BURGUNDY-STYLE WINE

Imperial	Metric	
4 pts.	2.25 l.	Burgundy-Type Grape Concentrate
1½ tsp.	1½ tsp.	Tannin
¼ tsp.	¼ tsp.	Pectic Enzyme
2 tsp.	2 tsp.	Yeast Nutrients
½ tsp.	½ tsp.	Yeast Energizer
1½ gal.	6.75 l.	Water
		Burgundy Yeast Starter

Add the tannin, pectic enzyme, nutrients and energizer to the water and stir vigorously until everything has completely dissolved. Blend in the grape concentrate, then inoculate the must with the actively fermenting yeast starter. Let fermentation continue undisturbed until no sugar remains and a dry wine is achieved. Leave the new wine to stand for about a week before racking it so that much of the suspended yeast and other debris can settle out. Add 1 fl. oz. (30 mls.) stock sulphite solution or the equivalent in crushed Campden tablets. Rack it for the second time in another 2 months or sooner if a thick deposit is observed. This wine will usually be clear and ready for bottling when its third racking falls due in another 3 months. Add ½ fl. oz. (15 mls.) stock sulphite solution or 2 crushed Campden tablets, then bottle the wine. Age it in bottle for a few months longer before serving as a red table wine.

RED BURGUNDY-STYLE WINE

Imperial	Metric	
1 pt	*570 mls*	*Red Burgundy-Type Grape Concentrate*
½ tsp.	*½ tsp.*	*Acid Blend*
¼ tsp.	*¼ tsp.*	*Tannin*
¼ tsp.	*¼ tsp.*	*Pectic Enzyme*
1 tsp.	*1 tsp.*	*Yeast Nutrients*
¼ tsp.	*¼ tsp.*	*Yeast Energizer*
8 ozs.	*225 gms.*	*Sugar*
6½ pts.	*3.75 l.*	*Water*
		Burgundy Yeast Starter

Mix the concentrate with about ½ gallon (2 litres) of water in which the nutrients, energizer, acid blend, tannin, pectic enzyme and sugar have already been dissolved. Add the balance of the water and introduce the actively fermenting yeast starter. Allow the must to ferment to dryness. Leave the new wine to clarify for about a week after fermentation comes to an end before racking it for the first time. Add ½ fl. oz. (15 mls.) stock sulphite solution or 2 crushed Campden tablets. Rack for the second time in another 2 months or as soon as a thick sediment is noticed. A third racking will be needed in another 3 months by which time the wine will usually be quite clear. Add ¼ fl. oz. (7 mls.) stock sulphite solution or 1 crushed Campden tablet at this point. Bottle the clear wine and let it age for another month or two in bottle before serving as a red table wine.

BURGUNDY-STYLE WINE

Imperial	Metric	
40 fl. ozs.	*1.13 l.*	*Burgundy-Type Grape Concentrate*
¼ tsp.	*¼ tsp.*	*Tannin*
¼ tsp.	*¼ tsp.*	*Pectic Enzyme*
¼ tsp.	*¼ tsp.*	*Yeast Energizer*
3 qts.	*3.5 l.*	*Water*
		Burgundy Yeast Starter

Dissolve the pectic enzyme, tannin and yeast energizer in the water then blend in the grape concentrate. Stir vigorously until it has completely gone into solution. Inoculate the must with the actively fermenting yeast starter. Allow fermentation to proceed undisturbed until the yeast has utilized all the sugar and a dry wine is obtained. Rack the new wine about a week after all yeast activity has ceased when much of the insoluble material in suspension will have settled out. Sulphite lightly with ½ fl. oz. (15 mls.) stock solution or 2 crushed Campden tablets. Rack again in a further 2 months or sooner if a thick deposit accumulates. This wine will generally be clear by the time its third racking falls due in another 3 months. Treat it with ¼ fl. oz. (7 mls.) stock sulphite solution or 1 crushed Campden tablet before bottling it. Set the bottles aside to age for a few months before serving.

CHIANTI-STYLE WINE

Imperial	Metric	
1 pt	*570 mls*	*Red Grape Concentrate*
4 ozs.	*110 gms.*	*Dried Elderberries*
¼ tsp.	*¼ tsp.*	*Pectic Enzyme*
1 tsp.	*1 tsp.*	*Yeast Nutrients*
¼ tsp.	*¼ tsp.*	*Yeast Energizer*
12 ozs.	*340 gms.*	*Sugar*
7 pts.	*4 l.*	*Water*
		General Purpose Yeast Starter

Add the pectic enzyme, nutrients, energizer and sugar to the water and stir vigorously until all these ingredients have completely dissolved. Mix in the grape concentrate, then inoculate the must with the actively fermenting yeast starter. Once fermentation commences, wash the dried elderberries with several changes of water to remove adhering dirt and preservative, adding a little sulphite solution to the final rinse to sterilize the fruit. Add the freshly washed fruit to the fermenting must. Ferment on the pulp for 3 days, then strain it off and discard it. Leave the must to finish fermenting and rack it for the first time about a week after all yeast activity comes to an end. Add ½ fl. oz. (15 mls.) stock sulphite solution or 2 crushed Campden tablets. Rack for the second time in another 2 months or sooner if a thick sediment settles out. This wine will normally be clear and ready for bottling by the time it is due for its third racking in a further 3 months. Add ¼ fl. oz. (7 mls.) stock sulphite solution or 1 crushed Campden tablet at this stage. Bottle the wine and let it mature in bottle for several more months before serving as a hearty red table wine.

CHIANTI-STYLE WINE

Imperial	Metric	
40 fl. ozs.	1.13 l.	Chianti-Type Grape Concentrate
1 tsp.	1 tsp.	Tannin
¼ tsp.	¼ tsp.	Pectic Enzyme
¼ tsp.	¼ tsp.	Yeast Energizer
3 qts.	3.5 l.	Water
		Chianti Yeast Starter

Mix the concentrate with the water in which all the other ingredients except the yeast starter have already been dissolved. Stir vigorously to ensure that the concentrate has completely dissolved. Introduce the actively fermenting yeast starter. Let fermentation continue until the yeast has utilized all the sugar and a dry wine is obtained. Leave the new wine to stand undisturbed for about a week so that much of the yeast and other insoluble material in suspension can settle out. Rack the wine at this point and add ½ fl. oz. (15 mls.) stock sulphite solution or 2 crushed Campden tablets. Rack for the second time in another 2 months or sooner if a large deposit is observed. This wine will normally be bright and clear by the time it is due for its third racking in a further 3 months. Add ¼ fl. oz. (7 mls.) stock sulphite solution or 1 crushed Campden tablet, then bottle the wine. Allow to age in bottle for several months before serving as a red table wine.

SAUTERNES-STYLE WINE

Imperial	Metric	
1 pt	570 mls	Sauternes-Type Grape Concentrate
¼ tsp.	¼ tsp.	Pectic Enzyme
¼ tsp.	¼ tsp.	Tannin
¼ tsp.	¼ tsp.	Yeast Energizer
12 ozs.	Sugar	240 gms.
6½ pts.	3.75 l.	Water
		Sauternes Yeast Starter

Dissolve the pectic enzyme, tannin, energizer and sugar in the water, then mix in the grape concentrate. Inoculate the must with the actively fermenting yeast starter. Allow the must to ferment to dryness. After all yeast activity has ceased, leave the new wine undisturbed for about a week to permit much of the suspended matter to settle out. Rack the wine at this point and add ½ fl. oz. (15 mls.) stock sulphite solution or 2 crushed Campden tablets. Rack it again after another 2 months or sooner if a heavy sediment accumulates. If this wine is still slightly hazy by the time the third racking falls due in a further 3 months, clarify it with the aid of a reliable proprietary fining agent. Sweeten it with ½ lb. (225 gms.) sugar, stirring vigorously until it has all dissolved, or add it in the form of a heavy syrup. Add ¼ fl. oz. (7 mls.) stock sulphite solution or 1 crushed Campden tablet together with ¼ tsp. stabilizer to prevent subsequent refermentation. Bottle the young wine and allow it to mature in bottle for another few months before serving well chilled.

SAUTERNES-STYLE WINE

Imperial	Metric	
1 pt	*570 mls*	*Sauternes-Type Grape Concentrate*
¾ tsp.	*¾ tsp.*	*Acid Blend*
¼ tsp.	*¼ tsp.*	*Tannin*
¼ tsp.	*¼ tsp.*	*Pectic Enzyme*
1 tsp.	*1 tsp.*	*Yeast Nutrients*
½ tsp.	*½ tsp.*	*Yeast Energizer*
6½ pts.	*3.75 l.*	*Water*
		Sugar as required
		Sauternes Yeast Starter

Dissolve the acid blend, pectic enzyme, tannin, nutrients, energizer and ½ lb. (225 gms.) sugar in the water, then add the grape concentrate and mix thoroughly. Introduce the actively fermenting yeast starter. Check the gravity regularly as fermentation proceeds until a reading of about 5 is recorded. At this point, add 4 ozs. (110 gms.) sugar, preferably in the form of a heavy syrup, and allow fermentation to continue. Repeat this procedure every time the gravity drops to 5 until fermentation finally comes to an end. Allow the wine to stand undisturbed for about a week after this point is reached before racking it for the first time. Add ½ fl. oz. (15 mls.) stock sulphite solution or

2 crushed Campden tablets. Rack again in another 2 months or sooner if a heavy sediment accumulates. This wine will usually be quite clear by the time its third racking falls due, but at times a faint residual haze may persist. In that case, clarify the wine with the aid of a reliable proprietary fining agent. Sweeten the clear wine to taste with a sugar syrup and add ¼ tsp. stabilizer or 1 crushed stabilizer tablet to prevent an inconvenient refermentation. Bottle the wine and set it aside for a few months to allow it to acquire some bottle age. Serve well chilled.

SWEET MUSCATEL WINE

Imperial	Metric	
1 pt	*570 mls*	*Muscatel Grape Concentrate*
1 tsp.	*1 tsp.*	*Acid Blend*
¼ tsp.	*¼ tsp.*	*Tannin*
¼ tsp.	*¼ tsp.*	*Pectic Enzyme*
1 tsp.	*1 tsp.*	*Yeast Nutrients*
½ tsp.	*½ tsp.*	*Yeast Energizer*
1 lb.	*450 gms.*	*Sugar*
6½ pts.	*3.75 l.*	*Water*
		General Purpose Yeast Starter

Add all the ingredients except the grape concentrate and yeast starter to the water and stir until they have all dissolved. Mix in the grape concentrate and stir vigorously before introducing the actively fermenting yeast starter. Allow fermentation to proceed until the yeast has utilized all the sugar and a dry wine is obtained. Rack the new wine for the first time about a week later and add ½ fl. oz. (15 mls.) stock sulphite solution or 2 crushed Campden tablets. A second racking will be required as soon as a heavy deposit builds up or after another 2 months if only a little sediment settles out. This wine will usually be bright and clear by the time the third racking falls due in another 3 months. Sweeten to taste with sugar syrup at this point, then add ¼ fl. oz. (7 mls.) stock sulphite solution or 1 crushed Campden tablet together with ¼ tsp. stabilizer to prevent any subsequent refermentation. Bottle the wine and age it in bottle for several months longer before serving it well chilled.

SWEET MUSCAT WINE

Imperial	Metric	
30 fl. ozs.	850 mls.	Spanish Muscatel Grape Concentrate
1 oz.	30 gms.	Acid Blend
1 tsp.	1 tsp.	Tannin
¼ tsp.	¼ tsp.	Pectic Enzyme
2 tsp.	2 tsp.	Yeast Nutrients
½ tsp.	½ tsp.	Yeast Energizer
1 lb.	450 gms.	Sugar
10 pts.	5.75 l.	Water
		Madeira Yeast Starter

Stand the can of concentrate in some hot water for about half an hour to thin the consistency of its contents. In the meantime, add the remaining ingredients except for the yeast starter to the water and stir vigorously until they have all completely dissolved. Mix in the grape concentrate and again stir vigorously for a few minutes. Introduce the actively fermenting yeast starter. Allow fermentation to proceed until no sugar remains and a dry wine is obtained. Leave the new wine to stand undisturbed for about a week after this stage is reached so that much of the material in suspension can settle out. Rack the new wine and add ½ fl. oz. (15 mls.) stock sulphite solution or 2 crushed Campden tablets. Rack it again as soon as a thick deposit is observed or after 2 months if only a small sediment accumulates. Should this wine still be hazy by the time its third racking falls due in another 3 months, clarify it with the aid of a reliable proprietary fining agent. Sweeten the clear wine to taste with sugar syrup and add ¼ tsp. stabilizer to prevent any subsequent refermentation. Bottle the wine and allow it to age for another month or two in bottle before serving lightly chilled.

RED DESSERT WINE

Imperial	Metric	
1 pt	570 mls	Red Grape Concentrate
8 fl. ozs.	225 mls.	Irish Elderberry Concentrate
¼ tsp.	¼ tsp.	Pectic Enzyme
1 tsp.	1 tsp.	Yeast Nutrients
¼ tsp.	¼ tsp.	Yeast Energizer
1 lb.	450 gms.	Sugar
6 pts.	3.5 l.	Water
		Port Yeast Starter

Blend the grape concentrate and elderberry concentrate with the water in which all the other ingredients except the yeast starter have already been dissolved. Inoculate the must with the actively fermenting yeast starter. Allow the must to ferment until no more sugar remains and a dry wine is obtained. Rack the new wine about a week later after much of the suspended yeast and other matter has settled to the bottom of the container. Add ½ fl. oz. (15 mls.) stock sulphite solution or 2 crushed Campden tablets. Leave the wine to stand undisturbed for another 2 months before racking it unless a thick sediment forms in a shorter time. Rack it for the third time in a further 3 months. Sweeten it to taste at this stage with sugar syrup, then add ¼ fl. oz. (7 mls.) stock sulphite solution together with ¼ tsp. stabilizer to prevent fermentation from restarting at a later date. Bottle the wine and leave it to age in bottle for a month or two longer before serving.

MEDIUM SHERRY-STYLE WINE

Imperial	Metric	
1 pt.	*570 mls.*	*Medium Sherry-Type Grape Concentrate*
1 oz.	*30 gms.*	*Gypsum*
¼ tsp.	*¼ tsp.*	*Pectic Enzyme*
1 tsp.	*1 tsp.*	*Yeast Nutrients*
½ tsp.	*½ tsp.*	*Yeast Energizer*
6 pts.	*3.5 l.*	*Water*
		Sugar as required
		Sherry Yeast Starter

Add the nutrients, energizer, pectic enzyme and 1lb. (450 gms.) sugar to the water and stir vigorously until all these ingredients have dissolved. Mix in the grape concentrate. Sprinkle the gypsum over the surface of the must, stirring it all the time during this operation so that the gypsum is properly distributed throughout the must. Excess gypsum will rapidly start settling out when stirring ceases, but enough will have reacted with the cream of tartar in the concentrate to have the desired effect. Inoculate the must with the actively fermenting yeast starter. Check the gravity periodically as fermentation proceeds until it drops to about 5. At this point, add 4 ozs. (110 gms.) sugar, preferably in the form of a strong syrup, and leave fermentation to continue. Repeat this procedure every time the gravity decreases to 5 until fermentation finally comes to an end. Rack the new wine about a week later and add ¼ fl. oz. (7 mls.) stock sulphite solution. Transfer it into smaller containers which are only about two-thirds full and age the wine there for several months to develop its sherry charcter. Do not rack it during this period unless a really heavy deposit builds up. Siphon the wine off its lees at the end of this time and sweeten it to taste with sugar syrup. Add 1 crushed stabilizer tablet and ¼ fl. oz. (7 mls.) stock sulphite solution, then bottle the wine. Serve delicately chilled.

CREAM SHERRY-STYLE WINE

Imperial	Metric	
1 pt	570 mls	Cream Sherry-Type Grape Concentrate
1 oz.	30 gms.	Gypsum
¼ tsp.	¼ tsp.	Pectic Enzyme
½ tsp.	½ tsp.	Yeast Energizer
6 pts.	3.5 l.	Water
		Sugar as required
		Sherry Yeast Starter

Dissolve the energizer and pectic enzyme together with 1 lb. (450 gms.) sugar, then blend in the grape concentrate. Sprinkle the gypsum over the surface of the must, stirring it all the time so that the gypsum is well dispersed throughout the must. Although much of this gypsum will settle out within a short time, enough of it will have reacted with the cream of tartar supplied by the concentrate to have the desired effect. Introduce the actively fermenting yeast starter. Once fermentation starts, check the gravity regularly until a reading of about 5 is recorded. At this point, add 4 ozs (110 gms.) sugar, preferably in the form of a heavy syrup, and allow fermentation to proceed. Continue checking the gravity and repeat this procedure every time it drops to around 5. When the fermentation finally does come to an end, leave the new wine to stand undisturbed for about a week to permit suspended matter to settle out. Rack the wine and add ¼ fl. oz. (7 mls.) stock sulphite solution or 1 crushed Campden tablet. Transfer it into smaller containers which are filled to only about two-thirds of their capacity and age it under these conditions for a few months without further racking. At the end of this time, rack the wine off its lees and sweeten it to taste with sugar syrup. Add ¼ tsp. stabilizer to prevent fermentation from recurring and bottle the wine.

CREAM SHERRY-STYLE WINE

Imperial	Metric	
1 pt	*570 mls*	*Cream Sherry-Type Grape Concentrate*
¼ oz.	*7 gms.*	*Cream of Tartar*
1 oz.	*30 gms.*	*Gypsum*
¼ tsp.	*¼ tsp.*	*Pectic Enzyme*
1 tsp.	*1 tsp.*	*Yeast Nutrients*
½ tsp.	*½ tsp.*	*Yeast Energizer*
6½ pts.	*3.75 l.*	*Water*
		Sugar as required
		Sherry Yeast Starter

Add the concentrate to the water in which the pectic enzyme, nutrients, energizer and 12 ozs. (350 gms.) sugar have already been dissolved and mix thoroughly. Add the cream of tartar and stir vigorously until it has completely dissolved (this will take a little time). Sprinkle the gypsum over the surface of the must with constant stirring and again mix well. Most of this gypsum will not appear to dissolve but an excess is needed to interact properly with the cream of tartar. After all these ingredients have been added, inoculate the must with the actively fermenting yeast starter. Allow fermentation to proceed until the gravity of the must drops to around 5. At this point, add 4 ozs. (110 gms.) sugar, preferably in the form of a heavy syrup, and allow the fermentation to continue. Keep on checking the gravity and repeat this procedure whenever a reading of 5 is recorded. When the yeast finally reaches its maximum alcohol tolerance and fermentation comes to an end, leave the new wine to clarify for about a week then rack it for the first time. Add ¼ fl. oz. (7 mls.) stock sulphite solution or 1 crushed Campden tablet. Transfer the wine into smaller containers which are filled to only about two-thirds of their capacity and age the wine there for a few months. No further racking should be carried out unless a heavy sediment accumulates. At the end of this time, rack the wine off its lees and, if necessary, clarify it with the aid of a reliable proprietary fining agent. Sweeten the clear wine to taste with sugar syrup and add ¼ tsp. stabilizer before bottling it.

PORT-STYLE WINE

Imperial	Metric	
1 pt	*570 mls*	*Port-Type Grape Concentrate*
¼ tsp.	*¼ tsp.*	*Tannin*
¼ tsp.	*¼ tsp.*	*Pectic Enzyme*
½ tsp.	*½ tsp.*	*Yeast Energizer*
6 pts	*3.5 l.*	*Water*
		Sugar as required
		Port Yeast Starter

Add the tannin, pectic enzyme, energizer and 1 lb. (450 gms.) sugar to the water and stir vigorously until everything has completely dissolved. Mix in the grape concentrate, then introduce the actively fermenting yeast starter. Allow the must to ferment until the gravity drops to around 5. At this point, add 4 ozs. (110 gms.) sugar, preferably in the form of a heavy syrup, and allow the fermentation to continue. Check the gravity regularly and repeat this procedure every time a reading of about 5 is recorded until the yeast finally reaches its maximum alcohol tolerance and fermentation ceases. Allow the new wine to stand undisturbed for about a week after this stage is reached, then rack it for the first time. Add ½ fl. oz. (15 mls.) stock sulphite solution or 2 crushed Campden tablets. Rack again as soon as a heavy deposit is observed or after 2 months if only a little sediment accumulates. This wine will usually be quite clear by the time the third racking falls due in another 3 months. Sweeten it to taste with sugar syrup at this point, then add ¼ fl. oz. (7 mls) stock sulphite solution or 1 crushed Campden tablet. Mix in ¼ tsp. stabilizer or 1 crushed stabilizer table to prevent subsequent refermentation. Bottle the wine and allow it to mature in bottle for at least some months longer.

PORT-STYLE WINE

Imperial	Metric	
1 pt	570 mls	Port-Type Grape Concentrate
¼ tsp.	¼ tsp.	Tannin
¼ tsp.	¼ tsp.	Pectic Enzyme
½ tsp.	½ tsp.	Yeast Energizer
6 pts	3.5 l.	Water
		Sugar as required
		Port Yeast Starter

Add the tannin, pectic enzyme, energizer and 1 lb. (450 gms.) sugar to the water and stir vigorously until everything has completely dissolved. Mix in the grape concentrate, then introduce the actively fermenting yeast starter. Allow the must to ferment until the gravity drops to around 5. At this point, add 4 ozs. (110 gms.) sugar, preferably in the form of a heavy syrup, and allow the fermentation to continue. Check the gravity regularly and repeat this procedure every time a reading of about 5 is recorded until the yeast finally reaches its maximum alcohol tolerance and fermentation ceases. Allow the new wine to stand undisturbed for about a week after this stage is reached, then rack it for the first time. Add ½ fl. oz. (15 mls.) stock sulphite solution or 2 crushed Campden tablets. Rack again as soon as a heavy deposit is observed or after 2 months if only a little sediment accumulates. This wine will usually be quite clear by the time the third racking falls due in another 3 months. Sweeten it to taste with sugar syrup at this point, then add ¼ fl. oz. (7 mls.) stock sulphite solution or 1 crushed Campden tablet. Mix in ¼ tsp. stabilizer or 1 crushed stabilizer tablet to prevent subsequent refermentation. Bottle the wine and allow it to mature in bottle for at least some months longer.

MADEIRA-STYLE WINE

Imperial	Metric	
1 pt	570 mls	Madeira-Type Grape Concentrate
1 tsp.	1 tsp.	Acid Blend
¼ tsp.	¼ tsp.	Tannin
¼ tsp.	¼ tsp.	Pectic Enzyme
1 tsp.	1 tsp.	Yeast Nutrients

½ tsp.	½ tsp.	*Yeast Energizer*
6 pts.	3.5 l.	*Water*
		Sugar as required
		Madeira Yeast Starter

Add all the ingredients except the yeast starter to the water and stir until everything has completely dissolved. Inoculate the must with the actively fermenting yeast starter. Once fermentation commences, add 1 lb. (450 gms.) sugar to the must and stir until it has gone into solution. Check the gravity regularly as fermentation proceeds until a reading of around 5 is recorded. At this point, add 4 ozs (110 gms.) sugar, preferably in the form of a heavy syrup, and let fermentation continue. Repeat this procedure every time the gravity drops to 5 until the must finally finishes fermenting because the yeast has reached its maximum alcohol tolerance. Rack the new wine about a week later and add ½ fl. oz. (15 mls.) stock sulphite solution or 2 crushed Campden tablets. Rack it again as soon as a heavy sediment is observed or after 2 months if only a small deposit forms. Sweeten the wine following the third racking in another 3 months, using either sugar syrup or honey. Add ¼ fl. oz. (7 mls.) stock sulphite solution or 1 crushed Campden tablet together with ¼ tsp. stabilizer to prevent fermentation from recurring. Bottle the wine and allow to age in bottle for another few months.

MADEIRA-STYLE WINE

Imperial	Metric	
1 pt.	570 mls.	*Madeira-Type Grape Concentrate*
½ tsp.	½ tsp.	*Tannin*
¼ tsp.	¼ tsp.	*Pectic Enzyme*
1 tsp.	1 tsp.	*Yeast Nutrients*
½ tsp.	½ tsp.	*Yeast Energizer*
6 pts.	3.5 l.	*Water*
		Sugar as required
		Madeira Yeast Starter

Dissolve the tannin, pectic enzyme, nutrients, energizer and 1½ lbs. (675 gms.) sugar in the water, then mix in the grape concentrate. Introduce the actively fermenting yeast starter. Check the gravity regularly during fermentation until it drops to around 5. At this stage, add 4 ozs (110 gms.) sugar, preferably in the form of a heavy syrup, and allow the fermentation to proceed. Repeat this procedure every time a gravity of about 5 is recorded until the yeast can no longer continue and fermentation finally finishes. Let the wine stand undisturbed for about another week, then rack it off the deposit of yeast and other insoluble matter. Add ½ fl. oz. (15 mls.) stock sulphite solution or 2 crushed Campden tablets. Rack it for the second time in another 2 months or sooner if a heavy deposit builds up. Following the third racking 3 months later, sweeten the wine with about 1 lb. (450 gms.) sugar and add ¼ fl. oz. (7 mls.) stock sulphite solution in conjunction with 1 crushed stabilizer tablet. Bottle the newly sweetened wine and allow it to mature in bottle for at least a few more months before serving it at the end of a fine dinner.

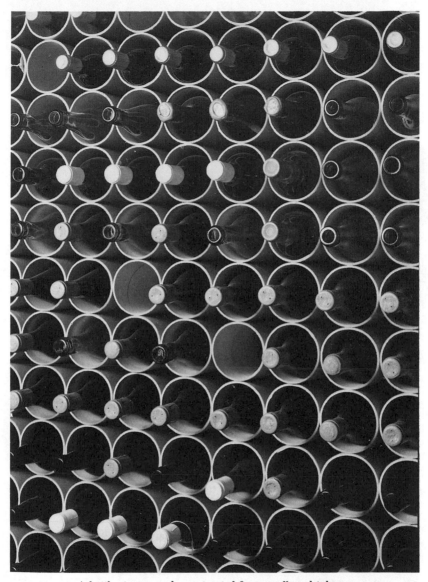

A bottle storage rack constructed from cardboard tubes.

INDEX

Acid
—Balance 20
—citric 38
—content36
—lactic 28
—malic 38
—tartaric 38
Acidity 38
Air lock 6
Alcohol 19

Bacteria 15
—Vinegar 27
Beaujolais-style Wine 71-73
Bordeaux 1
Bottles 5
Bouquet 33
Burgundy-style Wine 73-75

Campden tablets 14
Caramelization of sugars 30
Carbon dioxide 6
Chablis-style Wine 61
Champagne-style Wine 61-62
Chianti-style Wine 75-76
Claret-style Wine 68-71
Clarity 36
Cleaning 14
Clearing 24
Clear Wine 34
Colour extraction 31
Concentrates
—Frozen and canned fruits 41
—exotic canned fruit 43

—frozen orange 17-18, 43
-fruit juice 1, 41
-grape 1, 29, 31, 37-38
—making wine from 39
—sources of supply 36
Cream Sherry-style Wine 81-83

Dilution 35, 38
Distillation
—vacuum 30-32, 42

Earthenware Crocks 2
Enzymes 24-25,30
Ex-wine fives 5

Fermentation 2, 3, 19, 34
—vessels 2, 3
Fining agents 25
Flowers of wine 28
Freeze-drying 31, 42
French Vermouth-style Wine
47-48
Fruit Fly 15
Funnels 6

Glass carboy 2, 3, 4
Grape
—Arropes 32
—concentrate 1, 29, 32
—fresh 30
Graves-style Wine 58-60
Gravity 37
—tables 13

INDEX

haze 25
Hock-style Wine 54-56
Hydrometer 9, 11

Italian Vermouth-style Wine
49-50

J-tube 7, 24

Lead poisoning 2
Liebfraumilch-style Wine 58
Light Red Table Wine 66-67

Madeira-style Wine 84-86
Maturing 25
Medium Sherry-style Wine 80-81
Metal
—articles 2
—contamination 6
Methyl Hydrate 25
Moselle-style Wine 52-54

Off-flavours 28
Oxygen 26
Pale Sherry-style Wine 46-47
Pectin, Pectinol 24-25
Plastic
—containers 2-4
—tubing 7
Polyethylene 3
Port-style Wine 83-84

Potassium Metabisulphite 14
Practical aspects 34
Primary fermentation 3
Principles and practices 1

Racking 23
Raisins 35
Red Burgundy-style Wine 74
Red Dessert Wine 79-80
Red Table Wine 65-66, 67-68
Red Vermouth-style Wine 49
Rhine-style Wine 56-57
Rosé Table Wine 62-63, 64-65
Roseberry Rosé 63-64

Sauternes-style Wine 76-78
Siphoning 7 23
Specific gravity9
Spoilage 27
—containers 14, 15
Sterilizing
—containers 14, 15
—solution 14, 15, 24
Storage space 34-35
Sugar content 9
Sweet Muscat Wine 78
Sweet Muscatel Wine 79

Temperatures 20, 26
Toxic Pigments 3

White Port-style Wine 48

INDEX

White Table Wine 50-52
Wine
—imported 1
—vinegar 27
Wineries 1

Yeast
—baker's 16
—brewer's 16
—dried 16
—nutrients 18, 19
—starters 17-8